BARNDOMINIUM FLOOR PLANS AND DESIGNS 2024

From Blueprint to Bliss: Your Comprehensive 2024 Handbook for Floor Plans and Designs

Bryant A. Boughton

Copyright © 2023 Bryant A. Boughton- All rights reserved.

No part of this publication may be reproduced, stored in a retrieval system, or transmitted in any form or by any means, electronic, mechanical, photocopying, recording, or scanning, without permission in writing by the author.

CONTENTS

Introduction 1

Chapter 1

What is a Barndominium? 2

    History of the Barndominium 2

    Who Should Build a Barndominium? 3

    Barndominiums are built by who? 4

    What is a Barndominium Land Plot? 5

    What Kinds of Floor Plans Are Available for a Barndominium? 5

Chapter 2

5 Bedroom 2 Story Barndominium Floor Plans 6

    Top Barndominium Floor Plans For The Modern Barndo 9

Chapter 3

How to Frame a Barndominium 16

    Barndominium Financing Options 18

    Different Ways to Financing a Barndominium 18

    Barndominium-Specific Lenders 23

    Barndominium Financing Requirements 24

    Choosing the Right Barndominium Financing Option 26

    Tips for a Successful Barndominium Financing Application 28

Chapter 4

Things You Should Know About Building a Barndominium 31

    Big Black Barn Oklahoma has a 5700-square-foot barn with living space. 33

Chapter 5

Cozy Converted Barn Barndominium with Loads of Style 41

    Barndominium Interior Design Ideas 44

Barndominium Exterior Ideas You Will Love 53

Spacious Tennessee Barndominium | 2600 Sq Ft Living Space and a Huge Garage with Glass Door 55

Chapter 6

Mistakes to Avoid When Building Your Barndominium 63

Building a Barndominium in Colorado 65

Colorado Barndominium Financing 67

Chapter 7

Modern Farmhouse Plans with Barndominium Style 69

Barndominium Floor Plans 77

How many different kinds of basements can a barndominium have? 86

Chapter 8

Barndominium Garage Doors 89

Chapter 9

Garage Plans with Barndominium Style 93

What's the Difference Between a Pole Barn and a Barndominium? Three Good Reasons Why It's Better to Have Living Space and Storage in One Building 98

What's the Difference Between a Pole Barn and a Barndominium? 99

Chapter 10

How To Budget For Building A Barndominium 102

Advantages of Constructing a Barndominium 102

How to Fund Your Project for a Barndominium 106

Tips for Staying on Budget During Construction 108

Introduction

Our relationship with the spaces we name home is continuously changing, as seen by the growth of the barndominium in a world where traditional architectural limits are continually being challenged. The word "barndominium" is a portmanteau of the words "barn" and "condominium," and it refers to a structure that is both functional and inventive. This creative housing idea has seen a spectacular rise in popularity at the start of the twenty-first century, changing not only how we live but also how we think about home design.

You have received an exclusive invitation to embark on an architectural exploration and innovation adventure with "BARNDOMINIUM FLOOR PLANS AND DESIGNS 2024". We explore the core of the barndominium phenomenon in the pages of this thorough book, revealing the many opportunities it presents and the special charm it bestows on those who dare to use it.

Combining the Past and the Present

Originating from modest farming beginnings, the barndominium symbolizes a harmonious union of the past and the contemporary. It is, at its core, the spirit of ingenuity, sustainability, and flexibility that recalls a time when barns were essential to the survival of rural communities. Nonetheless, it skillfully combines modern functionality, design, and technology to satisfy the demands and preferences of modern living.

A Creativity Canvas

The adaptability of the barndominium is one of its most alluring features. It acts as a blank canvas where both architects and homeowners are free to express their ideas. We present a variety of exquisite designs in "BARNDOMINIUM FLOOR PLANS AND DESIGNS 2024," each of which has a distinct vision and personality. The alternatives are endless and range from spacious, open floor plans that make the most of natural light and space to comfortable, rustic hideaways that embrace the warmth of wood and exposed beams.

How to Live a Sustainable Life

The barndominium offers an option to live lightly on the planet in a time when sustainability is a top priority. This creative housing form is a great fit for eco-conscious living because of its strong metal framework, adaptability to existing barn buildings, and possibilities for energy-efficient design.

A Liberated and Expressive Way of Life

Embracing the unusual and eschewing convention is central to the barndominium lifestyle. It's about designing your living environment to suit your goals, interests, and requirements. The barndominium's natural adaptability invites you to express yourself in your living space, whether that means adding a sizable workshop, a greenhouse, or an enormous art studio.

Throughout "BARNDOMINIUM FLOOR PLANS AND DESIGNS 2024," you'll come across a delightful assortment of floor plans and design concepts that accommodate a wide range of tastes and inclinations. We provide you a thorough understanding of the interior design, construction factors, and architectural features.

Chapter 1

What is a Barndominium?

It seems like these days you can't read anything about homes or houses without coming across a book about the newest trends. If you've been paying attention to the new types of houses that are coming up, you may have heard of tiny homes, van homes, and shipping container homes. But the word you may have found by accident and been most amazed by is probably "barndominium." Even though the name is interesting on its own, you may also be interested in what it might mean. The word "barndominium" makes you think of many things, but what it really means and what it could do for you is even more interesting.

We have written this book to tell you everything you need to know about this cool and new way to build a house. If you know what a barndominium is and how it differs from other home trends, you might be able to decide if it's the right choice for you. We want you to be able to build any kind of home and make the right choice. You should know everything about it in order to do that.

What exactly is a Barndominium?

The word "barndominium" comes from the words "barn" and "condominium." Even though it's pretty clear, barndominiums are also known as "barndos" and "barn homes." The main idea is always the same, no matter what they are called. A barndominium is a house made from a metal barn, either brand new or used. This is important because barndominiums don't need the complicated wood frame and other building parts that a regular house does. They are put together with something called a post frame structure. With a post frame structure, it can be much easier to build a house than with a regular house frame.

Posts in a metal post frame building are driven into the ground instead of being built on top of each other and held up by them. Most barndominiums have a concrete block base that is put down first, and then the metal building is put on top of it. After that, the metal pole barn is built up on the inside, just like a house. The inside of barndominiums looks just like the inside of regular homes because of this. While looking at the inside of a barndominium, you would never be able to tell the difference between the two. One reason they're so famous is because of this. You can do almost anything you want on the inside, just like you would with a traditionally built home. They are easy to build. Finding out "what is a barndominium" is easy: it's just like a regular house, but it's much simpler to put together.

History of the Barndominium

There is nothing new about the idea of making a house inside a barn. People on farms often put their homes in or next to their stables so they could keep an eye on their animals at night. In this way, farmers could stay alert and not lose their way of life just because the work day was over. However, the word "barndominium" was first used in a book from 1989 in the New York Times. The book tells you "what is a barndominium?" and then goes on to talk about an equestrian community in Connecticut where people who wanted to live their lives around their horses could do so in houses that also had horse stables. This idea came from real estate developer Karl Nilsen, and the community became well-known for its unique ideas and concept.

After this first book in The New York Times, barndominiums didn't seem to be talked about much. That is, until an episode of Fixer Upper on HGTV, where the hosts turned an old barn into a modern, high-end house. This made people more interested in using metal post-frame buildings, which led to more requests for these kinds of homes to be built. Since then, they've been showing up all over the country, but the south is where they're most known. Barndominiums can be made in any type of location, though, and they can be useful for people who want to live in a one-of-a-kind home. "What is a barndominium?" is a question that people ask less and less often.

Who Should Build a Barndominium?

A barndominium might be a good choice for almost everyone, but there are some people who might really enjoy living in one. On the other hand, a barndominium might be the right choice for you if you want to make your house exactly how you want it. A barndominium is a type of home that can be customized in almost any way you want. If that sounds like something you'd be interested in, it might be a great fit for you. A barndominium is also usually cheaper because it doesn't take as much work to put it together. This gives a custom builder a lot of choices about what they can afford for their new house.

Another thing to think about is price. A barndominium could be a good choice for someone who can't normally afford the high cost of building a custom house. In general, building a barndominium is much less expensive than building a regular house. We will talk more about this later in the book. This means that people who are having trouble with their budget for a new home might be able to handle the lower cost of building a barndominium. This makes a custom home possible for people who are buying their first home or who haven't gone past the planning stage of building a custom home.

In what way is a barndominium built?

A metal post frame building kit is often used to build a barndominium. For those who are ready to take on the challenge, they can also be built from scratch. Concrete slab foundations are different from regular home foundations and can be a little easier to build and set. This is what most barndominiums are built on. The main difference between a barndominium and a regular house is that a barndominium does not have structural support like a house does. This means that the metal pole frame can be put together a lot faster than a regular house. This saves money and makes things easier for both the builder and the person who is ordering the building.

Different companies also sell barndominiums as kits that can be put together. With these kits, you have everything you need to build your barndominium. This is a great choice for people who don't want to start from scratch. Barndominium kits will come with clear instructions, and when it's time to put it together, you can often get help from the company that made it. The company that makes the kit will sometimes even send a licensed builder to your spot to put it together.

Barndominiums are built by who?

If you want to build your barndominium from scratch, you don't have to do it all by yourself. For many years, one of the bad things about barndominiums was that not many people knew how to put them together. Thankfully, that is no longer the case. A lot of builders now know how to build barndominiums because they are so popular. Some even make them as their main type of building. Over the course of a year, new builders all over the country show up who are skilled at putting up metal pole structures. Now that barndominiums are more common, builders are much less likely to ask you, "What is a barndominium?"

So, here are some things you should look for in a barndominium builder. Make sure the person you hire for the job has experience with projects like yours before. Plenty of different types of builders work in the industry, and some might not know how to put up a metal pole barn. You should also look for a builder who has good relationships with the people whose homes they have built in the past. You want someone to be on your side the whole time you're building a house because it's a very personal project.

Is it possible to get a loan for a barndominium?

A lot of people used to have a hard time getting loans for barndominiums, just like they did with builders. Most of the time, this was because banks didn't fully understand these kinds of homes and wouldn't be as ready to lend money for something they didn't fully understand. That has changed a lot, though, over the years. Less and less banks are asking what a barndominium is because they are becoming more and more popular. Most of the time, this is true in southern states where barndominiums are popular.

One thing you should look for in a bank that will lend you money for a barndominium is that they specialize in farming. This is especially important if you want to farm on your land. It is more likely that an agriculture bank will lend you money if they know that the project will fit in with the farming in the area. If you are just starting to build a barndominium, this might be a good place to start. It's also important to know about the right security for your barndominium insurance, along with how to finance your barndominium.

What is a Barndominium Land Plot?

When people ask what a barndominium is, one of the main things they want to know is how to get the right land for it. The most important thing is to find a piece of land that will work for your barndominium. You can look for land online in a lot of different places. The land you buy should be in the country enough that you have room to build your house, but not so far away that you can't get services there. Putting services on a lot can cost a lot of money, so it's best if the land you buy already has them.

Also, look for land that has been cleared enough for you to build on. Any land you find will need some cleaning, but not so much that it costs a lot of money to get rid of trees and other plants. It will save you a lot of time and money in the long run to build your barndominium on land that is already made ready.

What Kinds of Floor Plans Are Available for a Barndominium?

Your barndominium can have almost any type of floor plan you can think of. Simply put, you should be able to make any shape you want within the limits of a barndo's concrete slab base. A barndominium can have wraparound porches, more than one bedroom and bathroom, and a lot of other cool features. The only thing that stops you is your ideas. If you use barndominium planning software, it might be easier to plan your barndominium.

Types of Homes: Traditional and Barndominium

The price is the biggest difference between a barndominium and a regular house. Building a barndominium costs a lot less than building a regular house. This is because they are so much easy to set up. For a traditional house, the first phase of construction can take up to a year. It takes about 6 months to build a barndominium, though, if everything goes as planned.

Taking care of a barndominium is different from taking care of a regular house in another important way. There is a lot of wood used to build traditional houses. Things like rot, mold, and mildew can grow on them because of this. This won't be a problem with a barndominium because they are mostly made of metal and will hold up well against weather like wind, rain, and ice.

In conclusion

You can start your barndominium off on the right foot if you know what it is and how it is different from a regular house. There are many good things about a barndominium and almost no bad things about how it is built. You can now choose if one of these beautiful, one-of-a-kind homes is right for you and your family now that you know what it takes to build one and how the whole process works.

Chapter 2

5 Bedroom 2 Story Barndominium Floor Plans

Flexibility is undoubtedly one of the advantages of a two-story, five-bedroom house plan. These house plans feature open floor layouts and, of course, the adorable curb appeal of a barndominium, which is currently very in style. Take a look at these five-bedroom, two-story barndominium floor designs.

Floor Plan for a Barndominium with Five Bedrooms and Two Stories

Floor plan for a barndominium with two stories, five bedrooms, and a front outside

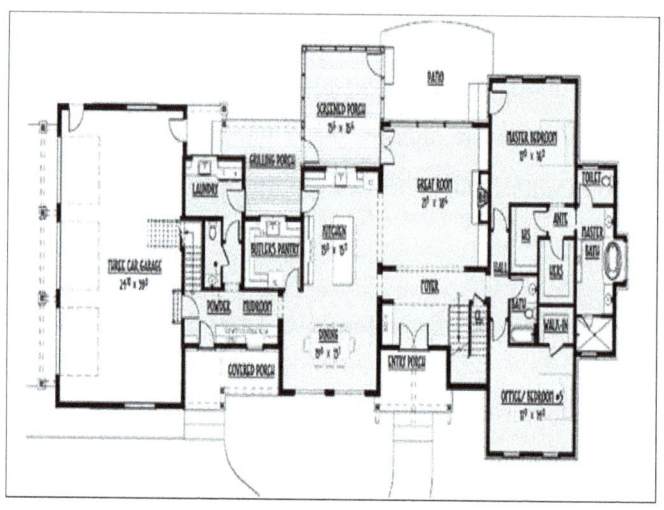

Main Floor Plan for a Two-Story Barndominium with Five Bedrooms

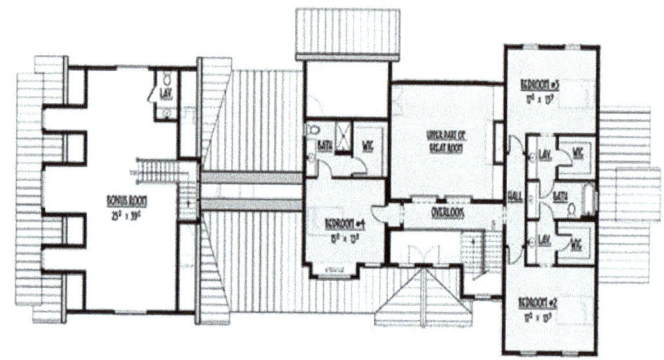

The upper floor plan of a two-story barndominium with five bedrooms

This classic five-bedroom barndominium has stone veneer accents, board-and-batten siding, and gables. This floor design is made more elegant by the entryway and front porch. Through the entrance, a contemporary open plan and a breathtaking view of the backyard are unveiled, complimented by wide windows. These windows, which span the entire two levels of the barndominium layout, are really striking. Situated on the ground floor, the main suite offers two walk-in closets, a complete bathroom with a tub, and a rear patio access. There's also a guest bedroom on the first floor, which doubles as a home office.

There are three guest bedrooms upstairs on the second story, each with a large walk-in closet. Views of the great room below are also available from the walkway that leads to the guest suites.

Floor plan of a two-story, five-bedroom barndominium with an in-law suite

Floor Plan for a 5-Bedroom, 2-Story Barndominium with an In-Law Suite and Front Exterior

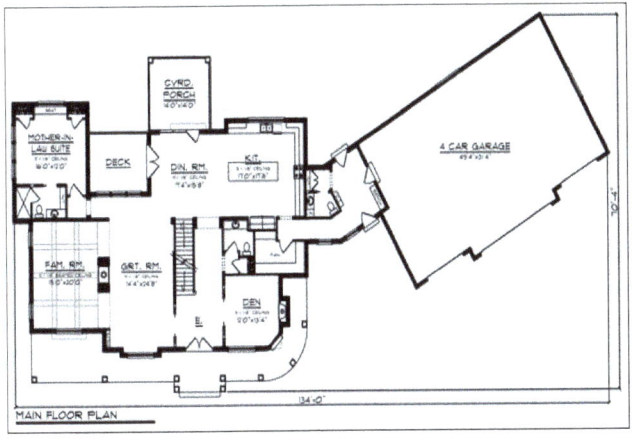

Main Floor Plan of a Two-Story Barndominium with Five Bedrooms and an In-Law Suite

Floor plan for a two-story, five-bedroom barndominium with an in-law suite on the upper floor

The first level of this two-story barndominium floor plan has an in-law suite, adding to the home's adaptability. A two-way fireplace separates the two sitting spaces of the formal family room, which is adjacent to the in-law suite. For any relatives who live in, having a separate in-law suite on the first floor is perfect. Three guest bedrooms are located upstairs, each with easy access to the laundry room and a walk-in closet. Situated on the second level, the opulent primary suite boasts an astounding walk-in closet.

Vintage two-story barndominium floor plan with five bedrooms

Traditional Two-Story Barndominium Floor Plan with Five Bedrooms - Front Exterior

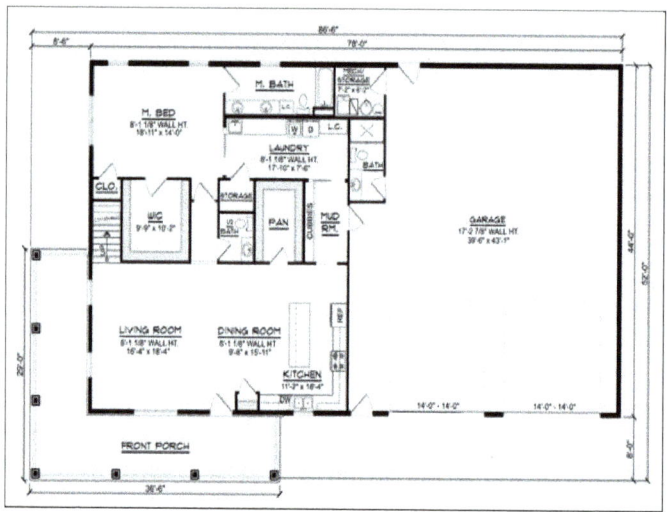

Main Floor Plan of a Traditional Two-Story Barndominium with Five Bedrooms

Stunning 2-story, 5-bedroom barndominium with a front outside

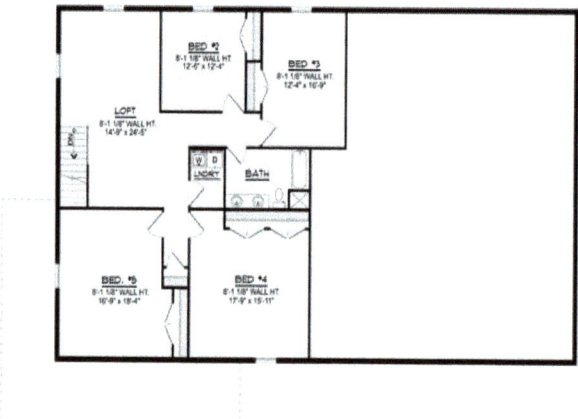

Traditional Two-Story Barndominium Floor Plan with Five Bedrooms - Upper Floor Plan

This two-story barndominium plan's spacious two-car garage is what draws our attention to it right away. Larger cars and equipment may be stored in the two-car garage thanks to the raised ceilings and space for a workshop. There's a handy mud room on the first floor that leads through the garage to the walk-in laundry room. The primary suite, which has a walk-in closet and a private bathroom, is connected to the laundry area. The second floor houses the second laundry area, the comfortable loft, and all of the guest bedrooms.

Special two-story barndominium with five bedrooms

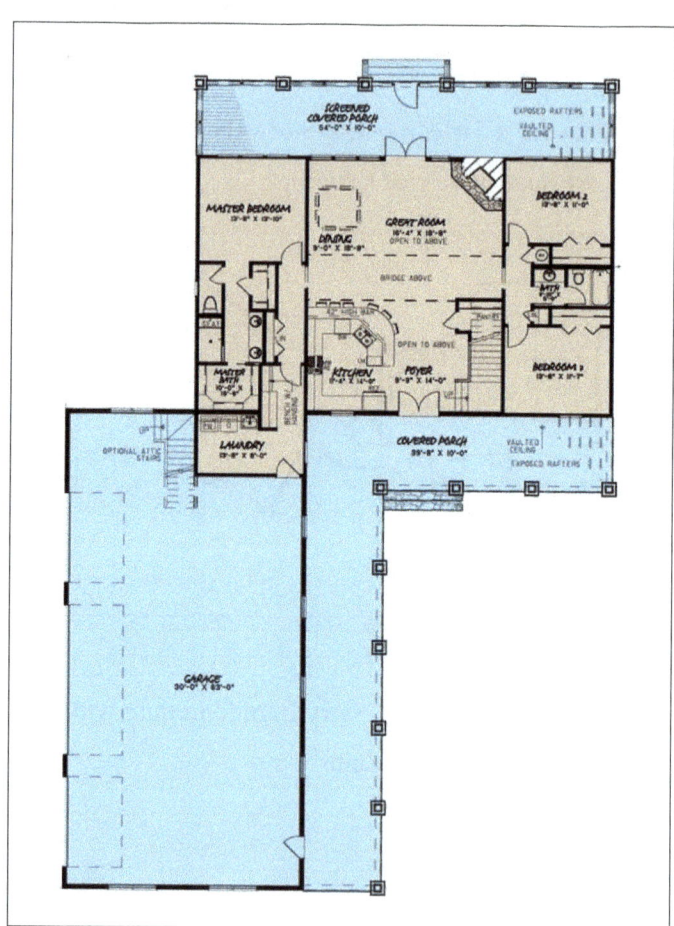

Special Two-Story Barndominium with Five Bedrooms - Main Floor Plan

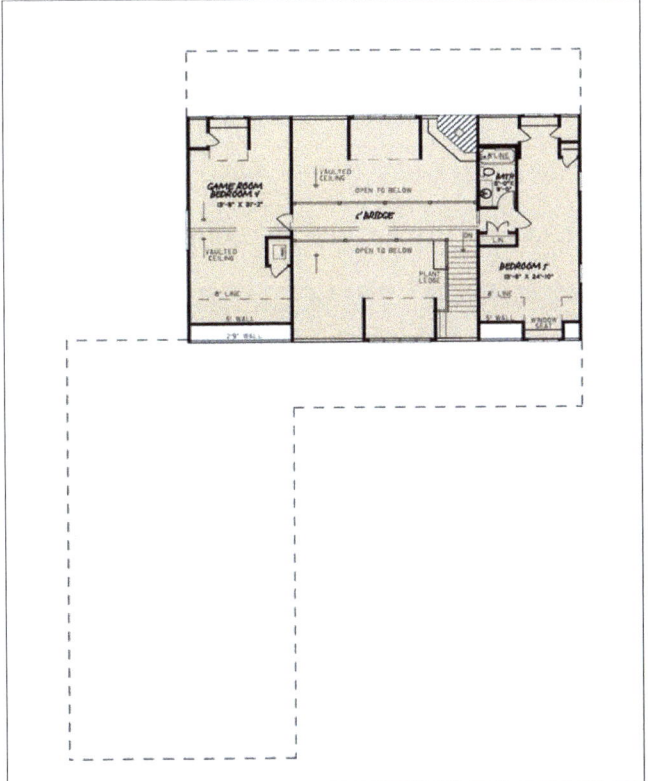

Stunning Two-Story Barndominium with Five Bedrooms - Upper Floor Plan

This L-shaped barndominium floor plan has a covered porch that gives it a really charming rural exterior. The four-car garage is completely enclosed by a porch. Located on the first level, across from the two guest bedrooms, is the main suite. The open living area, with its outstanding indoor-outdoor flow to the rear porch, divides the bedrooms. The two last guest bedrooms on the second level have an unusual arrangement where a bridge connects them. The bedrooms themselves have plenty of extra storage space in addition to being very roomy.

Top Barndominium Floor Plans For The Modern Barndo

Barndominium floor plans, also referred to as "barndo" floor plans, are rustic, steel-framed, or barn-inspired residences. They provide tastefully constructed homes with all the modern conveniences of a functioning home, including a distinctive external design and an expansive garage or workshop space.

Barndominiums, which were once created for architectural uses like storing hay, grains, fruits, and the farm's cattle, have grown to be among the most inventive housing designs.

How the Barndominium Evolved

It wasn't until Chip and Joanna Gaines converted a barn into a house in the third season of Fixer Upper that the word "barndominium" and the concept of living in a barn-style home gained traction. Before becoming popular throughout the rest of the nation, the style garnered a lot of attention in Texas, Oklahoma, and other southern states. It did away with the notion of really living with horses and made a garage/workshop a prominent component.

Barndominiums became more and more popular as a result of the affordability of this home style being recognized by both builders and house plan designers. You can see how the top 20 barndominium floor plans provide thoughtfully planned homes with excellent curb appeal and essential features to suit any size family as you look through them.

Features of Condominium Houses

One of the most imaginative and motivational home designs are barn house ideas. Barndominiums are becoming more and more popular. They are closely tied to the architectural features of the Modern Farmhouse, which is one of the most popular house types in this industry's history.

Plans for Barn Houses Are Special

When you envision a historic barn being converted into a home, you would envision the interior design of the home to incorporate all the traditional features. Floor plans for barndominiums retain the personality and charm of the architecture while mirroring the unique features of a conventional barn. All of our designs use contemporary elements to create a cozy and useful home. a blend of board and batten, steel, and rustic siding. The rectangular shape, gabled roof, elongated porches, and barn-style doors and windows are typical features of these house plans. Our interiors usually have an open floor plan to emulate the light and airy feel of a classic barn. They also have lofts, exposed beams for decoration, and very high ceilings.

The Sizes Of Barndominiums Are Varying

Our barn house plans come in a variety of sizes to meet the demands of the homeowner. Those seeking a smaller footprint might choose from the smallest barndos, which are slightly under 1,200 square feet. The largest of the barndos is 4,913 square feet.The barndominium floor plans provide a wide choice of house designs and features depending on your demands and the needs of your family. Take a look at the selection of the greatest barn house plans below, for instance, which showcase the finest craftsmanship, elegant features, and useful layouts.

The Top 20 Floor Plans for Barndominiums

20. Design 963-00660 - "The Chic Barndo"

The ultra-modern Plan 963-00660 is one of thenewest additions to the barndominium designs collection. This unusual house plan is surrounded by large windows that let in an abundance of natural light. This three-bedroom plan, with its black façade, offers 2,752 square feet, 2.5 bathrooms, an open concept layout, a mudroom, and an office.

19."The Exclusive Barndo" plan 5032-00140

Five bedrooms, three bathrooms, an open floor plan, a loft, and an office are all included in Plan 5032-00140.

18."A Barndo Dripping with Sophistication" is the plan number 963-00625.

Who would have thought that the words "barn" and "sophisticated" would be used together? However, there's no way to characterize this house layout as anything less. The interior's isquare footage of elegant finishes is inspired by its three bedrooms, two bathrooms, divided bedrooms, open concept layout, loft, and office.

17. Layout 963-00432: "Very Nice Garage!"

This barndo has an amazing 3,570 square foot garage and uses various materials to enhance its architectural façade! In addition, Plan 963-00432 includes 2,776 square feet, four bedrooms, three bathrooms, a loft, and cathedral ceilings.

16. "The Sunny Barndo," Plan 963-00602

This rustic beauty, which is one of the 3-bedroom barn home designs, has a large sunroom with a cathedral ceiling and a fireplace. This house plan features a three-car garage, an open floor plan, and two bathrooms.

15. Plan 5032-00136: "A Workshop and Barndo"

A well-thought-out floor design featuring numerous discrete leisure spaces and a garage workshop is found in design 5032-00136. With 2,765 square feet, two bedrooms, two full bathrooms, and a loft, this two-story barndominium is spacious. Check out our special 360° tour of this plan for a close-up, intimate look at the floor plan!

14. "The Rectangular Barndo," Plan No. 963-00644

Plan 963-00644, which forms a perfect rectangle, greets you with a sizable covered front porch. The porch and the interior of the house are all decorated with cathedral ceilings. In addition, there are three bedrooms, two bathrooms, split bedrooms, and an open floor plan within its 1,695 square foot interior.

13. The "A Barndo with Garage Storage" plan, number 5032-00117

This may be the layout for you if you're searching for a well-thought-out barndominium floor plan with space for your RV or boat. Three bedrooms, 2.5 bathrooms, an open floor plan, a large wrap-around porch, a loft, and an office are all included in Plan 5032-00117. Enter these 2,456 square feet. ft. layout with our premium 360° tour to see the expansive 1,280 square foot parking area.

12. "The Red Barndo," Plan 8318-00115

This open-concept barndominium features a covered patio with a tall window wall to lighten the interior and distinctive glass garage doors. This two-story barndominium floor plan, which has the master suite on the main floor, has 2,079 square feet with 3 bedrooms, 2.5 bathrooms, and a loft. There are also 1,164 square feet set aside for the garage.

10. "A Barndo for an RV" is Plan 5032-00152.

This one-story barn home plan has a main front entry and a broad covered porch, modeled after the rustic red color of a traditional barn. With Plan 8318-00115, 3,277 sq. ft., an open floor plan, divided bedrooms, five bedrooms, 3.5 bathrooms, and a mudroom.

11. "The Ranch Style Barndominium," Plan 963-00387

For individuals who require room for an RV, this industrial house plan is the ideal size. Not to mention a half bathroom, the garage is a spacious 1,480 square feet. Plan 5032-00152 has 2,311 square feet on the interior, with 3 bedrooms, 2.5 bathrooms, a wrap-around porch, a loft, and a mudroom.

9. "The Small Barndo," Plan 963-00601

Plan 963-00601, a well-liked 1,460-square-foot layout, demonstrates that larger isn't necessarily better. There are moments when only the necessities will do. Plans 963-00601, which have an open floor layout, two bedrooms, and a garage workshop, are all included.

8. "A Barndo with Outdoor Living Space," Plan 9401-00114

Plan 041-00260 is a timeless beauty that gives a nostalgic tribute to modest country living. This two-story barndominium plan features an open floor plan, a loft, a mudroom, and a big 2,992 square foot home design with four bedrooms and three bathrooms.

6. Scheme 6849-00064 - "The Opulent Barndo"

This stunning 2,486 square foot house plan makes optimal use of every square inch of space. Plan 9401-00114 features an open floor plan, three bedrooms, 2.5 bathrooms, a mudroom, an outdoor kitchen, and a study, so no space is left unexplored. Take a look at the 360° tour to explore this thoughtfully designed layout.

7. Scheme 041-00260 - "The Traditional Barndo"

Among the many distinctive elements of the amazing 4,357 square foot plan are a butler's pantry, a pet kennel, additional storage areas, and a workshop. In addition to having five bedrooms, this barn home plan has an open floor plan, four full bathrooms, two half bathrooms, a loft, a media room, a mudroom, and a library.

5. "The Apartment Barndo," Plan No. 963-00411

3. "The Metal Barn House Plan," Plan 5032-00010

The adaptable 2-bedroom barndominium floor plan, known as Plan 963-00411, is situated as an apartment over a 1,554 square foot garage. The top floor features an open floor plan with one bathroom and two bedrooms. In addition to room for two cars and an RV, the garage also has a mudroom and a half bathroom. This design is excellent for use as a primary home, an investment property, or a terrific spot to host adult children who are in need of housing.

Consumers have found Plan 5032-00010 to be quite popular due to its metal cladding and practicality. This two-story, 2,160-square-foot design has four bedrooms, 2.5 bathrooms, a loft, an open concept layout, and a mudroom in addition to a guest bedroom.

2. Design 5032-00119: "The Encircling Barndo"

4. "The Lakehouse Barndo," Plan 963-00627

This two-story barndominium, with its covered wrap-around porch and windows all around, would be a fantastic lake house. Soaring ceiling heights, four bedrooms, 3.5 bathrooms, an open floor plan, a sizable bonus room, a loft, and a mudroom are all aspects of the 3,205 square foot interior.

This popular floor design maximizes both interior and outdoor living areas. The front porch is covered and wraps around with ease! A porch that wraps around offers a ton of area for outdoor living. In addition, the garage has three car spaces, a workshop with access to a half bathroom, and storage. The interior, which has an open floor plan, 3 bedrooms, 2.5 bathrooms, a den, and a loft, makes outstanding use of its 2,765 square feet. Use the 360° tour to learn even more about this floor plan!

1. Known as "The Most Popular Barn," Plan 5032-00151

Best-selling barndominium, Plan 5032-00151, is exquisitely constructed of various materials with a hint of classic crimson. This charming barndo design features a large 2,123 square foot garage with an RV bay and enough for a workshop, in addition to its appealing wrap-around porch. The inside features three bedrooms, two bathrooms, an open floor plan, and cathedral ceilings. This house plan also has an alternative basement foundation and a loft over the garage. Take a 360° tour to appreciate this barn floor plan up close!

An inside 360-degree photo of Plan 5032-00151

In summary

Which of the best barndominium floor plans that you've learned about is your favorite now? Collection of barndominium floor plans is expanding, ranging from compact barndo floor plans to over 4,000 square feet.

Chapter 3

How to Frame a Barndominium

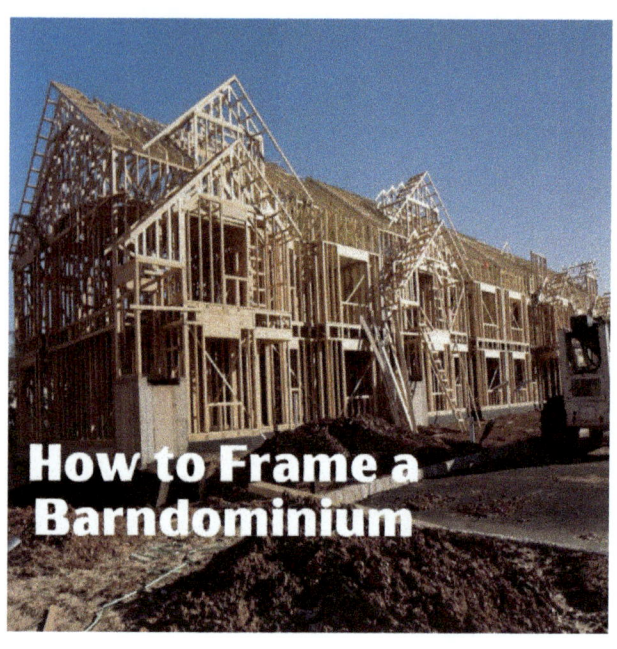

A barndominium's framing is an important part of the building process that you can try to do yourself. If you know how to do things yourself, you might be able to frame the inside of your barndominium.

Inside a barndominium, the walls are usually made of wood, just like inside a regular house. If you're making a barndominium instead of a regular house, the steps are a little different.

This guide will show you the basic steps you need to take to make a barndominium.

Set up the outer frames.

Before you can make a barndominium, you have to build the outside frames. Large steel frames are often used to build barndominiums. Along the inside walls' outside edges, wood frames are attached to the steel frame. For the drywall and the rest of the inner frame to stay in place, you need a wood frame.

When you start working on the inside frame, the flooring should already be in place. Put each frame down on the ground. The frame is made of 2x4 or 2x6 boards and is shaped like a square. Each 16 to 24 inches, 8-foot studs that have already been cut are added vertically.

Blocking gives the studs more support and keeps them from bending. When blocking, pieces of wood are put between the bolts on a horizontal plane. Add the horizontal boards about three to four feet below the frame's bottom.

Usually, the frame is put together in pieces that are each 10 feet wide. You build an 8-by-10-foot frame, raise it, and attach it to the steel frame around the outside and the base. Beginning in the middle and working your way out, begin in a corner of the inside.

Frame the doors and windows.

Frames for the windows and doors are usually added with extra 2x4 or 2x6 boards. To hold up a window or door, the screws are cut to fit a rectangular frame. The framing and siding on the outside should already be cut to fit the doors and windows.

New studs are put in on the door or window's left and right sides. Studs are cut to fit a board along the bottom of the frame when window frames are being put up.

Build the frames interior.

Once the outside walls are framed, you can move on to the inside. It's likely that you will use plans, which have details about the floor plan.

Beginning in a corner of the living room is always advised. For the inside walls, build the frames first, then the frames for the drawers and other features.

The inner frames are usually built on the floor, just like the outer frames. Lift the first frame of the wall and attach it to the outside frame. Keep going inside and making your way through.

Insert joists to create a second floor or mezzanine.

A single floor with a high, open roof is typical for barndominiums. You may need to put in ceiling beams and joists if your plans call for a second floor or a loft. At the tops of the wall frames, joists are put across the width of them.

Usually, sets of two 2x4s spread about 12 inches apart hold up the upper floor. Beyond the joists is a flooring. The inside walls of the top floor can be framed after the joists and subfloor have been put in.

Put in fittings for electrical and plumbing work

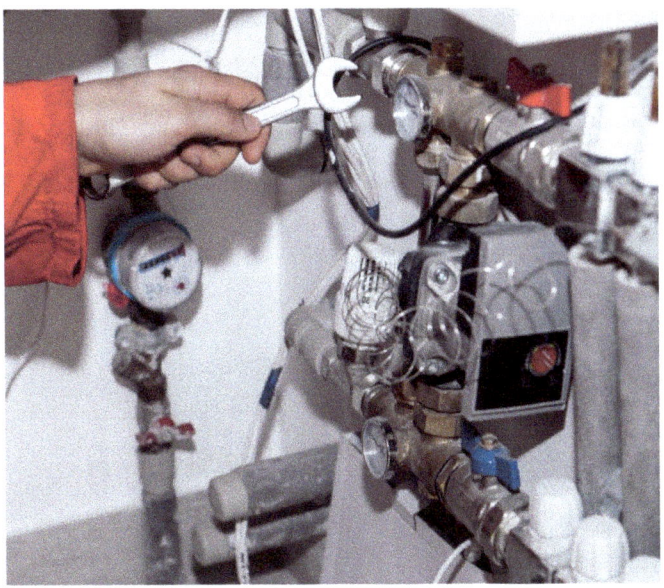

Fittings are needed for both the electrical and water work. You need to include electricity boxes and different plumbing parts. Quite often, the plugs have to be put in certain places.

For instance, you might need to make sure that all of the plugs are 12 to 18 inches above the ground. Also, in some places you have to put light switches 48 to 54 inches above the floor. If you're going to build the barndominium yourself, check your city's building rules first.

Finish up the inside of a barndominium

Once the fittings are in place, the inside of the barndominium is finished being framed. Still, there are a few steps left to finish the inside:

- Put in walls and insulation
- Cover and paint the ceiling and walls
- Put in flooring
- Put in the appliances and fittings

After the frame is finished, insulation and walls are put in. The easiest type of insulation to put in is batt insulation. It's sold in rolls that fit between the outside wall plates. Fiberboard insulation, which is cut to fit and put into the wall spaces, is another option.

You have to hang the walls before you can put in blown-in or spray foam insulation. Also, you might want to hire professionals to put in blown-in or spray foam. Both types of insulation need to be carefully put in place to make sure they cover everything.

Walls and ceilings are covered with drywall. When hanging drywall, you should always begin at the top. Two people or a drywall jack are needed to hang the drywall from the ceiling. To keep it from breaking, you need to make sure that the drywall is properly attached to the ceiling joists.

Start at the top of the wall and place the sheets of drywall horizontally instead of vertically when you hang them on the wall. Before you start on the bottom row, finish the top row around the walls.

When the plaster is done, you can paint the inside or put down flooring. It's possible to damage the paint job when putting in the floors if you paint the walls first. You could get paint on the new floors if you put them down first.

A lot of the time, fixtures and appliances are added last. Adding covers for light switches and outlets, ceiling lights, ceiling fans, and appliances are some of these finishing touches.

It's also common to wait to finish the kitchen and bathrooms until the frame is done. Recently, the countertops, fridge, and shelves were added to the barndominium.

How to Put Together the Frame of a Barndominium

Depending on the size of your floor plan, framing the inside of a barndominium could take a few weeks. Remember to begin with the outside walls first, as they will hold the rest of the frame. Start in one corner and finish the walls before framing the closets when building the inner frames.

You might want to hire a professional if any of the steps look too hard. It might be less likely for flaws or mistakes to happen if you pay a little more to hire someone else. Building a barndominium will still cost less than building a regular house, even if you hire a builder. This is because building a metal home takes less time when done right.

Barndominium Financing Options

Imagine that you want to find a cheap house in the country, away from the city. The best choice in that case is a barndominium, also called a "barndo."

A barndo is usually a single-family modular home with a permanent base and a big, open first floor that can be used for office space, hobbies, or just plain living.

Because of the way it's built, a barndo can stand on its own, with all of its power coming from its walls. Because of this, you can put up non-structural walls anywhere inside the shell to make the second floor bigger for living or sleeping.

Even though a barndo is less expensive than a regular house, many people still can't afford to buy one. Because of this, getting financing is an important part of buying it, and you should look at all of your choices.

Different Ways to Financing a Barndominium

Buy with cash

Some lucky people can buy their land with cash and don't have to worry about getting loans to build a barn. The pros and cons are presented below:

Pros

- You have full ownership of your home.
- You do not have to wait for an investor to decide if you are a good risk.
- No one cares about your credit score.
- As the market changes, you don't have to worry about interest rates going up.
- You can do whatever you want with your property as long as you follow the local building codes and zoning rules.

Cons

- All of your money is stuck in the house, which could mean that you don't have enough saved for other things.

Typical home loan loans

Because a standard mortgage loan isn't backed by the federal or state government, you make a deal with a lender based on your own skills. Conventional mortgage loans usually cost less and have better interest rates than other types of loans.

To be eligible, you usually need good credit and a down payment. You can expect high interest rates and a big down payment if you have bad credit, though.

A standard mortgage usually lets you borrow up to about $650,000. But the limit is about $980,000 if you're building in a high-cost place. But if you get a Jumbo loan, you can borrow more money.

Pros

- The rates on these loans are usually lower than those on other loans.
- If you have good credit, you might be able to get a mortgage with a flexible rate or one that only pays the interest.

Cons

- If you want the best interest rates, you need to have great credit.
- The amount of the down payment is based on your credit score. A low score means you need to put down a lot of money.
- A mortgage backed by the federal government or a state doesn't give you any extra perks.

Building loan programs

They have a higher interest rate than a regular home loan and are only good for a short time. For example, you can use it to buy land, buy building supplies, and pay a builder.

The money is sent to you at set times to pay for the building, and you only pay interest on what you've used. The loan changes to a regular long-term loan with regular mortgage interest rates when the building part is over.

You can get two different kinds of building loans:

Just building stuff

This loan really does work like it sounds. It's only for building up the land. Once the building is done, you'll need to find a regular debt to pay off the construction loan.

It's too bad that there will be two applications, two loans, and two closings. But you can look around for the best credit deal at any given time.

Pros

- You have more freedom to choose the best plan to pay off the loan.

- The borrowing rates might have gone down while the house was being built.

Cons

- This loan only pays for the building part.
- Mortgage rates may have gone up while the house was being built.
- There are two loans to talk about, and each one has its own closing costs.

Building to Permanent

Most debtors prefer this loan because they only have to deal with one loan and one set of closing costs. Before the work begins, the lender accepts the builder, the building plans, and the estimate.

The borrower usually only has to pay interest on the money the builder takes out at certain points in the project. About once every three to six months.

After the building phase is over and all the construction money has been used, the loan turns into a normal mortgage.

Pros

- There's just one loan to talk about.
- You only pay one closing fee.
- That one lender will help you the whole time.

Cons

- You are locked into the deal and can't get a regular mortgage from another company with better terms.

FHA Loans

Banks and private lenders offer the FHA loan as a way to get credit. The loan is backed by the Federal Housing Administration. Low- to moderate-income people, especially first-time sellers, can get help with home loans through this program.

The loan covers everything you need to buy a house, including land, materials, labor, and building permits. An FHA loan also has a low down payment requirement of 3.5%, which makes it a great option for people who can't afford to put down a lot of money.

The debt-to-income ratio is strict, but you can work with it if you have property or savings.

Pros

- The down payment must be at least 3.5%.
- There is no upper limit on income, so people with bad credit who make a lot of money can still apply.
- Available to people with bad credit. In most cases, you need at least a 580 score. If your score is between 500 and 579, though, you can still get a loan with a bigger down payment.
- Available for a variety of living types, such as barndominiums.
- Get low PRMI (Private Mortgage Insurance), even if you have bad credit.

Cons

- You can buy a single-family home for up to $472,030 in 2023, or $1,089,300 in places where homes are expensive.
- On top of your monthly mortgage payments, you have to pay a one-time insurance fee equal to 1.75 percent of the loan amount.
- You can only use an FHA loan to buy your main home. For investment or vacation homes, you need a different kind of loan.
- The home you buy has to meet strict safety standards, which can be hard to do if you're getting

something that needs work. The building has to be inspected to see if it meets the requirements before it can be qualified. Furthermore, any problems must be fixed before the loan is granted.

VA Loans

Let's say you are a military veteran or are currently serving. If so, you can refinance your current mortgage loan or buy a primary residence with one of the home loans made expressly for you by the Department of Veteran Affairs.

Your property is appraised by the VA to make sure it satisfies its minimal property criteria. You can conclude the loan once all approvals from the underwriters have been received.

To be eligible for a VA loan, you have to meet certain requirements. However, you can buy the property once you have the VA Home Loan Certificate of Eligibility.

Pros

- Mortgage insurance is not required for VA loans.
- There is no down payment required.
- Compared to a traditional loan, the interest rates are cheaper.
- No minimum credit score is necessary.
- VA loans facilitate the purchase of larger or more expensive homes by permitting a higher debt-to-income ratio.
- The VA caps the closing cost amount that a lender may impose at 1% of the loan amount.

Cons:

- The kind of property you can purchase is limited.
- Manufactured homes are subject to increased inspection and require a structural engineering examination.
- Real estate must be occupied by the owner.

- The asset needs to be used as a principal dwelling.
- Before purchasing, a house inspection and appraisal are required. As a result, many sellers will decline an offer from a seasoned buyer.
- A funding fee needs to be paid at closing. The fee is usually 2.15% of the total loan amount. You might not be required to pay this charge, though, if you are a surviving spouse or have a disability related to your military service.

USDA Loans

Numerous banks and commercial lenders have provided government-backed house loans to the US Department of Agriculture (USDA). Nevertheless, only specific rural areas are eligible for these loans.

The mortgage is available to low-income households and requires no down payment. Moreover, the application process is streamlined.

Let's say you would want to construct rather than purchase. In that instance, it offers a construction-to-permanent loan, which combines a mortgage and a construction loan into a single package with a single closing cost. The interest rate is typically in the range of 3.75%.

The property has the following requirements:

1. There needs to be a year-round access road to the property.
2. It needs to have a solid structure.
3. It needs to have a roof that works.
4. The property needs to have installed appropriate drainage and plumbing systems.
5. It needs to have an HVAC system that is up and running.
6. Its electrical system needs to be reliable and safe.

Pros

- There is no cap on guaranteed loans.
- No initial payment.
- The seller may be responsible for covering the closing costs. Either purchase a home or refinance an existing loan.
- Direct loans have fixed, low interest rates.

Cons:

- It has to be the primary residence.
- It must remain in a specific location.
- Your salary has to be within a specific range.
- There are one-time and upfront costs.
- The home cannot be used as a commercial investment. Yet, structures that were formerly commercial property can be purchased.
- To construct a new barndo, you must work with a contractor approved by the USDA.

House equity loans

Let's assume that your home loan still has worth. As such, you may pledge this as collateral for a loan to construct a barndominium.

Pros

- The loan's interest rate is predetermined and typically lower than others.
- Simple monthly installment plan.
- You can repay the loan over a maximum of 30 years.
- Nearly anything can be done with the loan.
- Interest payments could be deductible from taxes.

Cons:

- To be eligible for the loan, you must possess a sufficient portion of your current residence and retain above 15% of your total worth when the loan is repaid.
- There is a range of close costs from 2% to 5% of the loan amount.
- Taking on additional debt can reduce your available cash flow if you currently have one.
- A manageable debt to income ratio.
- Raise your credit rating to 660.
- A stellar credit history.
- Require evidence of a stable work.

Personal Loans

With personal loans, you can take out a loan for any reason. You pay back the loan with interest over a predetermined period of time.

Generally speaking, the maximum amount you can borrow is $100,000 spread over 12 years, subject to your credit and financial situation. Since personal loans are not secured, their interest rates are greater than those of secured loans.

Interest rates on personal loans are typically 9% for consumers whose credit scores are higher than 760.

Pros

The following are the benefits:

- Unlike payday loans and other short-term loans, you get a lump sum at a set monthly rate, which makes repayment easier to handle.
- The approval process for personal loans is quick. They are therefore useful in situations where you have to locate a large sum of money immediately, usually the following working day.
- Your house, car, or other assets are not pledged as collateral for a personal loan. As a result, in the event that you are unable to make the payments, you need not fear losing your house.

- The interest rates on personal loans are lower than those on credit cards. As of August 2023, the average interest rate on a personal loan was 11.29%, and the average interest rate on a credit card was 20.6%.
- In comparison to a credit card, you can apply for a larger loan amount.
- A personal loan can be used for any purpose. But before you take out the loan, find out if there are any usage restrictions from the lender.

Cons:

- Since the loan is unsecured, missing payments will have an adverse effect on your credit history and lower your credit score.
- A court may permit the lender to seize your assets if you are unable to repay the loan.
- High interest rates are typically assessed by the lender if your credit score is low.
- There are stringent qualifying standards for personal loans. You might therefore experience issues if your credit score is low and your credit history is bad.
- If you pay off the loan before the end of the term, fees and prepayment penalties may greatly raise the total cost of borrowing.
- In addition to credit card and mortgage payments, another consistent monthly obligation is a personal loan. As a result, you might have trouble sticking to your budget and making the required payments on time.
- Over the course of a fixed loan term, personal loans have higher fixed monthly installments. As a result, it's frequently harder to handle than credit cards with no late fees and a modest minimum monthly repayment requirement.

Barndominium-Specific Lenders

Barndos are typically classified as modular dwellings manufactured in factories that are assembled on-site. As a result, pick lenders who provide financing for modular homes—more especially, barndominiums.

The banks listed below have goods that are appropriate for barndos. There are plenty more, though, so look around and choose one that works for you. The list is solely arranged alphabetically.

(JP Morgan Chase & Co.) Chase Bank

One of the biggest lenders of mortgages in the United States is Chase Bank, formerly JP Morgan Chase & Co. Regretfully, their products likewise require the greatest standards.

Typically, a 20% down payment and a credit score of at least 700. However, for the chosen applicant, the business additionally provides fair interest rates.

In addition, they provide financing for modular homes that come with a credit line, letting you pay the builder and supplies gradually. You convert the construction loan into a regular mortgage at the conclusion of the construction phase, at which point interest is due.

Fairway Independent Mortgage

Among the biggest lenders in the United States is Fairway Independent Mortgage. A wide range of items, particularly barndo kits, are available for them. There are, however, few products appropriate for purchasing land and no construction financing available.

Down payments are 0% and credit scores higher than 580.

FMC Lending

You can get items fit for a barndominium from FMC Lending regardless of your credit score. On the other hand, you will pay higher interest rates and be required to make a down payment if your credit score is low.

Interest rates typically vary from 7.99% to 10.99%, while down payments often fall between 20% and 25%. If this is only for the first year of construction, it won't be too horrible. But it can get very expensive if stretched out over 15 or 20 years.

Flagstar

Numerous financing for modular homes are available from Flagstar Bank, some of which let you to buy the Barndo kit and put it together yourself. The land is also for sale. In every state, this company provides barndo financing.

A minimum credit score of 620 is required; down payments begin at 3%.

Go Mortgage Company

Go Mortgage Corporation provides a means of buying your property and barndo.

Various goods are offered based on your tastes and situation, so you may select the one that works best for you. Additionally, you don't pay interest on your loan until after you've moved in and the one-year build period has ended.

Minimum credit score of 640 and 3.5% down payment

National Home Loans

One of the best lenders for newly constructed barndos is Nationwide Home Loans Inc. But they only provide loans over $250,000. Therefore, people who wish to purchase a Barndo kit and self-build may find it inappropriate.

On the other hand, they provide flexible construction loans with a 12-month build period, and the interest is not charged until after you move in.

You can take out a loan to buy an existing property and a modular home. However, you require a credit score higher than 620. Some goods, meanwhile, don't demand a down payment.

Barndominium Financing Requirements

If you wish to receive an offer for a house loan, you must fulfill the lender's conditions. Generally speaking, using a program supported by the federal government will result in better terms than going it alone.

Below is a summary of the most important prerequisites.

Credit Score

Lenders use your creditworthiness to determine your level of financial risk. The degree to which you will honor the terms of your loan and repay it depends in part on your credit score and credit history.

A loan with a reduced interest rate is more likely to be approved for someone with a strong credit score of at least 650.

You need to have a score higher than 620 to apply for a typical home loan. Additionally, it will be easier the higher the score.

For a loan with a 10% down payment, you only need a score of 500–579 if you utilize one of the government-backed programs, such the FHA. Alternatively, the down payment is lowered to 3.5% with a score of 580 or higher.

Debt-to-Income Ratio

Having a healthy debt-to-income ratio is another prerequisite. The lender calculates how easy you can make the monthly payments by comparing your income and debts.

You must thus demonstrate that your salary covers both the additional debt and your living expenses.

Credit Reports

Equifax, Experian, and TransUnion are the three credit agencies that provide information about your past debt commitments and repayment performance.

These reports are used by lenders to assess your ability to make timely loan repayments.

Income and Employment History

You need documentation of your employment and income. Your ability to pay off your monthly bills must be consistently demonstrated to the lender.

In addition, the lender needs documentation proving your identity. For example, a regular monthly paycheck or tax return demonstrates your right to work in the nation and your promise not to use the loan for money laundering.

Collateral

Certain loan kinds, including home equity loans, call for collateral as a down payment. Usually, assets like real estate, vehicles, or savings accounts are used for this.

Because the lender is less likely to lose money on a secured loan than on an unsecured loan, interest rates on this sort of loan will be lower.

Downpayment

When a borrower takes out a loan, most lenders need a down payment. By requesting a down payment, you can lower the total amount borrowed and demonstrate to the lender that you are serious about the financing.

The down payment for a home loan is deposited into an escrow account overseen by a real estate attorney if you plan to purchase a property. The money is kept in the account and is paid to the seller after the sale is completed.

Property Appraisal

A lender needs to know how much your property is worth before determining how much to lend. The recent sales in the same area will determine this amount.

An appraiser looks at the property's condition, location, and similar home values before producing an appraiser's report.

This is the challenging part of buying a barndo. Because barndominiums are still a very uncommon type of modular home, there may not be enough of them in your area for the appraiser to draw a reasonable conclusion about their value.

Construction Plan and Budget

A home loan lender needs to know that you have planned your new-build barndo project thoroughly and that you have an approximate budget and timetable. The lender will then be better able to determine how much and how long you need to borrow.

You have to look professional, thus your presentation needs to be strong. Hire a qualified architect or a contractor who has been approved by your lender to provide credibility to your project.

Additionally, hiring a contractor who has already collaborated with the lender guarantees that the bank is aware that your barndo will be constructed expertly.

Choosing the Right Barndominium Financing Option

To obtain the best value for your money, select the appropriate barndo financing option from the appropriate institution.

Some things to think about while selecting a lender are listed in the list below.

Customer service

You need to be aware of all the procedures involved in borrowing money.

As a result, pick a lender that will communicate with you and answer your inquiries clearly and succinctly.

Rates of interest and terms

Examine the terms of the loans, down payments, and interest rates offered by various lenders.

Select the loan that best fits your needs based on the information provided.

For what fees are you liable?

As we already know, there are additional expenses and charges related to a home loan beyond of the mortgage repayments.

Thus, let us be cautious about the following:

fees of origination

These charges take care of your loan's administrative expenses.

Commissions.

Mortgage brokers are examples of third parties who receive commissions.

Lenders will occasionally cover this. However, it is typically covered by the borrower as part of the repayments or as an additional expense.

Credit report costs

A credit report from one of the credit bureaus is required by the lender. The expenses related to this are covered by this fee.

Once more, this can be paid either separately or as part of the monthly repayment schedule.

Points of discount

The borrower can lower their interest rate by making a one-time payment.

Expertise

It is not a good idea to choose a lender who has no knowledge with barndos in specific or modular homes in general. If you do, you will wind up purchasing an unsatisfactory product at a premium price.

Unaware of barndos, lenders will protect themselves by providing absurd terms and rates just to be safe.

Credibility

Don't enter this financial arrangement with blind hands. It is imperative that you ascertain the reputation of the lender.

As a result, check through customer evaluations to make sure they have a solid track record of customer satisfaction and are aware of what their clients want.

Selecting a loan option: Benefits and Drawbacks

You need to take the following factors into account when choosing a financing option, like a mortgage, to purchase a barndo:

Fixed-rate versus adjustable-rate home loans

It's easy to distinguish the two. While variable-rate loans have variable interest rates, fixed-rate loans have fixed rates.

If you can afford a short-term mortgage, then go for a variable-rate mortgage. Additionally, it is preferable to select a variable rate if the interest rate is continually declining; if it is rising, it is better to select a fixed rate.

Loan duration

Since a construction loan has a set short-term duration of one year, there is little you can do about it. On the other hand, a home loan may have a 15- or 30-year term.

If you can afford it, go for a 15-year loan with a higher monthly payment. However, you accelerate the debt payback and equity growth.

On the other hand, a 30-year loan has much smaller monthly payments, so people with lower incomes would find it more appropriate. On the other hand, paying interest over a 30-year period results in higher interest rates and a larger total amount.

Type of Loan

Numerous mortgage products are offered by banks and other lenders. The most popular mortgages, nevertheless, are the ones listed below.

- In accordance with current market conditions, a commercial bank provides conventional mortgages.
- Large loans are those that exceed $510,400. Talk to private investors if this is something you should do.
- To encourage low-income households to become homeowners, the federal government backs a portion of mortgage loans. The back loans from current lenders are FHA, VA, and USDA. These house loans are worth choosing if you fit the requirements because they are more reasonable, don't require a good credit score, and some don't require down payments.
- No-document loans do not require the standard credit score or documentation proving one's income. The down payment and interest rates, however, may be unaffordable for the average person. Additionally, not many lenders provide these.

Downpayment

It is preferable to put down as much as you can afford, even though some people may find it difficult to give a down payment.

Consequently, you take on less debt and pay less interest rates.

Penalties for prepayment

Should you be able to settle your house loan early, lenders will impose a prepayment penalty. By encouraging the borrower to spread out the principal repayment over a longer time frame, the penalty enables the lender to maximize interest revenue.

The penalty is often equal to the interest you were able to avoid paying. Thus, there is rarely a need to pay back a loan early.

Tips for a Successful Barndominium Financing Application

Make sure you adhere to the instructions below to increase your chances of success with your Barndo home loan.

Making the correct mistakes can shorten the application process and increase the likelihood that your application will be accepted.

Locate the ideal lender

Obtaining a traditional home loan is not the same as financing a barndo construct.

Select a lender who understands what a barndominium is and specializes in agricultural or modular construction.

Develop a sound plan.

The lender loves to read a clear, succinct report that outlines your needs for the money since it shows them that their money is in capable hands.

A solid plan should contain as much information as possible about the project you want to develop, the estimated cost of construction, the schedule, and the contractor you want to work with.

Put charts and pictures in there and give the impression that you are an expert. You'll be half way there if you provide this data in an elegant report that meets your needs.

Property evaluation

Consult a certified property appraiser to find out how much your land and completed project are worth.

Your finished property's appraiser may have difficulty estimating its value if there aren't enough barndos in the region. Don't give up though.

Are you able to get a mortgage?

Prior to searching for lenders, real estate, or barndo kits, you should ascertain how much you can afford to borrow.

You can find out about how much you can afford to repay when your bank or credit union examines your income and credit history.

Federal programs for home loans

Make sure you meet the requirements for any government-backed home loan program you plan to choose.

No matter how much money you have, you cannot enroll in the program if you are ineligible.

Boost your credit rating

Pay off the debts you now owe, particularly the larger ones.

As a result, both your residual income and your chances of being approved for a loan will rise.

Boost your earnings and savings

If you can, find a better paying career, relocate, or take on a part-time work to supplement your income. Another option is to use a high-interest savings account to augment the value of your current savings.

Attempt to cut back on your outgoings concurrently. Maybe look for alternate vacation spots and reduce the luxury.

Select a lender with experience funding barndominium purchases.

Particularly in rural locations, a lot of lenders specialize in barndominiums or modular homes.

Use some of the lenders included in this book, or get in touch with the USDA and other government home loan programs, which offer a list of approved lenders. Next, make contact with as many as you can to find out if they offer financing for barndominiums.

Prepare any necessary paperwork.

Obtain a copy of your credit report and review it for any inaccuracies or omissions. You'd be shocked at how many have inaccurate information.

Thus, sort them out right away. Your credit report will be provided to the lender, but they will also require supporting documentation to refute any mistakes that may still remain.

To make it easier for them to read, compile all the accompanying documentation for your application. The lender will frequently make things easier for you if you make it easy for them.

Collaborate with a knowledgeable barndominium builder

Put together your favorite builder's resume and appropriate references. Ascertain if they are qualified to work in your state and include copies of their license and insurance bond.

The lender will feel more at ease if you use a builder they already recommend or who has experience working on government home loan programs.

Answers to Common Questions

Common queries include the following:

How much does it usually cost to create a barndominium?

A barndo in 2022 cost between $120,000 and $540,000, with the average cost to build a 2,400 square foot one being about $300,000. This information comes from HomeAdvisor.

What is the required down payment for financing a barndominium?

The down payment required for a mortgage on a barndominium varies depending on the loan type, the lender, the construction site, and whether the loan is backed by a federal program.

The majority of lenders often demand a down payment of 20% or more of the total loan amount. On the other hand, there is no down payment needed for VA home loans.

When renting out a barndominium, is it possible?

In theory, a barndo can be rented out.

In actuality, though, this is dependent upon the mortgage conditions and financing requirements.

How long does it take to receive financing approval for a barndominium?

You should anticipate receiving an approval for your mortgage application from the underwriter in 45 days if all the necessary paperwork is in order and there are no delays.

Can someone with poor credit acquire a barndominium loan?

Individuals with low credit ratings can apply for house loans from a number of mortgage firms. On the other hand, budget for high interest rates and a sizeable down payment.

Alternatively, you can obtain a mortgage with a credit score of 500 if you qualify for one of the federal government home loan programs; some even waive the down payment requirement.

Next Actions

In order to qualify for a loan for a barndominium, you need to have the following:

- A solid credit history and score.
- An appropriate debt-to-income ratio.
- Enough money for closing costs and the down payment.
- Evidence of a consistent income.

Alternatively, take advantage of the better loan conditions offered by the VA, USDA, or FHA-backed federal home loan programs.

Certain homeowners think financing for a barndominium is complicated. However, it is identical to obtaining a traditional mortgage. If you take the time to learn about the criteria of the several lenders that provide barndo financing choices, you should have no trouble submitting your application. Why don't you act sooner?

Chapter 4

Things You Should Know About Building a Barndominium

If you love the outdoors and anything that looks like a barn, then living in a barndominium might be perfect for you.

Now tell me what a barndominium is. It's a huge building that's either an open-concept steel building built from the ground up or a barn that has been turned into a house. This kind of building is usually put up on a piece of land in rural areas with lots of land, but it's also starting to show up in places outside of cities.

Barndominiums are easier to build, last longer, and need less maintenance than standard wood-framed houses. They are also faster and cheaper to build.

But before you join the crowd and start building, whether it's on an already-built barn or a brand-new kit, you should do some study. These are the most important things you should know about making a barndominium.

1. **Get an approval for your project.**

To make sure everything is up to code, anyone starting a building job or remodeling must get the right permits. If you want to build a barndominium, you should set aside money for permits, which can range anywhere from $400 to $2,000 based on where you live.

The building and safety department in your area will probably have rules about the size and style of your building, as well as how to place a septic tank, wire it, and do the plumbing.

If the house you want to buy already has a barn on it, don't assume that it was built according to the rules or with the right permits. Talk to the planning office in your area to find out what changes you can and cannot make to your barn.

2. **Check the paint.**

It's important to find out what kind of finishes were used on an older barn before you fix it up.

Matt K., says that windows, walls, trim, siding, and other parts of older barns that were built before 1978 may have lead paint on them.

These places might be damaged during the renovation, so they need to be checked out before the work starts. Kunz says that the cost to fix the problem can be very high, depending on the size of the barn, if the test comes back positive.

3. Get ready for unexpected costs

It costs a lot less to build or fix up a barn to live in than it does to build a regular house. However, unexpected costs will still come up during the building process.

Don't forget how much it will cost to clear the land and get it ready for building. Also, you might need to build a new foundation. This can cost anywhere from $5,000 to $30,000, depending on where you live and the type of footing you need.

You're turning a building that's usually empty into a place to live, so you'll need to set aside money for current features that will make it feel like home. In this group are things like HVAC, tile or hardwood floors, and washer and dryer connections.

4. Make a plan for electricity work

Electricity is not something that needs to be thought about for a simple barn. But a barndominium needs electricity to work, so it's important to think about what kind of energy it will need early on.

You should hire a qualified and experienced electrical company and have them look over the power needs of all the lights and appliances that will be put in the house. The company should also make sure that all of the wires are in the exact spot where you want them to be.

Sean says, "It takes a lot more work to fix things after the Sheetrock or walls are up."

It can be hard to decide what kind of lighting to use and how to install it, so make your choices early to make sure they'll be available when it's time to install. As part of your makeover, you might also want to add smart doorbells, thermostats, and security lights or devices.

It can be pricey to make changes to a project after the contract has been signed.

5. Make smart choices about your doors and windows.

Drafty windows and doors are often the cause of high energy costs. And to keep your energy bill from going up, pick front doors made of fiberglass or heated steel and windows with two or three panes.

Brad Roberson, president of Glass Doctor, says that you should include a sliding glass door in your design to let more natural light into your home and enjoy life both indoors and outdoors.

"Look for composite gaskets, double-pane glass, and other features designed for energy efficiency," says Roberson when you are shopping for a sliding glass door.

6. **It's important to add soundproofing.**

Barndominiums aren't good at keeping a steady temperature because they are made with steel frames and metal walls. They can gain heat in the summer and lose heat in the winter.

To fix this problem, experts say to use batting as insulation or foam boards, insulated panels, or spray foam insulation to make things more resistant to heat.

Big Black Barn Oklahoma has a 5700-square-foot barn with living space.

More and more people want to build barndominiums, so those who want to won't have to worry about when to plan or start building. When barndominiums first came out, it was hard to find makers and get money to pay for them. There are a lot of builders today who also know a lot about barndominiums. Even people who work as interior designers would love to work with people who own barndominiums.

Take a seat and enjoy your coffee or tea. The Big Black Barn Oklahoma Barndominium, the home we're showing you today, will amaze you. There's not a single thing about this barn home that you won't enjoy. The upstairs has three rooms for living, a full bathroom with a walk-in closet, and a balcony. The basement is mostly the barn. There is 5700 square feet of covered room upstairs and downstairs.

Plus, a builder and a designer pair own it with their young family. That's great. What could be better?

Oklahoma Barndominium Outside

The family calls it "Big Black Barn." This house is a haven. It was built by Tray and planned by his wife, Brett McPherson. The iron ore color on the outside is kept on some parts of the outside, like the posts, beams, windows, and barn door. The difference is beautiful!

You'll first walk through the patio, where the family often hangs out, before you get to the inside. The porch is a cozy place for the owner to enjoy a drink or some coffee, read a book, or just chill out while watching the kids play. You can already tell what style the owner likes from this area.

Pops of color from throw pillows, plants, and a few one-of-a-kind pieces make that willow furniture look very rugged.

Black Barn Front Door

The floor plan of this house is very convenient, especially since the owners planned the barndo themselves. When you walk into the Big Black Barn Oklahoma Barndominium living room, you'll find yourself in a small kitchen. People who work in the barn won't have to go upstairs, which is handy. Even though it's small, it has everything you need, like a fridge, microwave, and even an ice maker, which adds a more modern touch to the Scandinavian style we'll see more of upstairs.

The black storage cabinets, white tabletop and backsplash, and brown floor tiles in the shape of polygons all go together perfectly. Different cooking items have fun pops of color and patterns that try to catch your eye.

There is a place to store muddy boots and horse hats around the corner from the small kitchen, right next to the door. There is also a bathroom in the area right at the bottom of the stairs. There is another door that leads to the alley of the barn.

We go up the stairs...

If the designs below made your eyes happy, get ready to enjoy every color, pattern, and accent the next level has to offer. In the Big Black Barn Oklahoma Barndominium, you can find more great design ideas. And each and every part has a story to tell.

I mean, who doesn't like stories? Every house is unique, and the stories that go along with it make it even more so. And to really show how much love and work the owners put into this beautiful home and to give you ideas, you'll hear some of those stories.

Begin with the stairs. Everyone takes great pride in their steps, and Brett loves going to all of them. So much light comes in through a big window. The picture below the window was Brett's first art purchase. It's one of the many things he loves about this small space. And in another corner would be a stack of pictures of their babies wearing Indian headdresses when they were born.

Not to leave anything out, these beautiful floor tiles add a little extra something to the landing of the stairs. Next, we'll talk about the extra-white paint job inside, which makes the whole room look very bright.

Now we'll go to the main living area!

You can come right in through those cool-looking batwing doors. From this point, the kitchen, living room, and eating area are all connected by a large open space. The Big Black Barn Oklahoma Barndominium has 1780 square feet of living room on the second floor, plus an 80-square-foot balcony. The kitchen and bathroom downstairs add up to 2100 square feet of living space.

Now, let's start to enjoy beauty more, shall we?

The kitchen

That's fine, you can have your quiet time. Take it all in. We both think the same thing. This green kitchen is wonderful. It's not very big, but it has black stainless-steel appliances and just the right amount of room (wait until I tell you about the cabinet tower in the corner)!

I do know that. The tiles on the wall. The lights and open shelves. The black farm sink and the window. The shades! Friends, no words. Take a few deep breaths and swoon!

Brett talks about her favorite things about the kitchen, like the black sink. Every day, her kids do arts and crafts on the white quartz counter. I like open shelves because they look good and are useful. We love this idea because these make it so easy to grab things and put them away.

Brett says that the tower on the right will save your life. The cabinet where she keeps the coffee pot, baby bottles, and other things is the most useful in the whole kitchen. P.S.

Big drawers hold pots and pans, paper plates, and cups. Everywhere else on the bottom level, there are rollouts that let you pull out a spice rack and a small, thin cabinet for cookie sheets.

In one corner is the eating area, and a door leads to the balcony.

Room for Living

Well, there are two places in this beautiful house where I can pretty much only say "wow" or "OMG." Not making this up. You will almost be unable to say anything about these designs and pieces.

There's a lot of empty space, so your eyes will jump from one thing to another. Each piece is deserving of praise. It has a lot of different Scandinavian styles mixed in with western and Native American touches. Pay special attention to the bright western arts, Pendleton patterns, tooled leather, and head mounts!

Some pieces in the Big Black Barn Oklahoma Barndominium, on the other hand, really stand out and have stories to tell. For example, the owners of the chandelier worked with two antler design companies to make this beautiful one-of-a-kind piece.

You must also be interested in those beautiful Big Black Barn Oklahoma Barndominium doors. All of the doors are made to order from slab doors with moldings applied and edges cut to fit. People are excited about everything, even the Kudu barn door handles.

Have these beautiful pieces already made your eyes happy? Here's one more! The room is inspired by the green giant swivel chairs that were made just for it. The people who own them will swear that these are just as cozy as they look.

The room is very bright and seems to go on forever because it is all white. Add in the light that the dome gives off. The knotty hardwood flooring, which looks old and worn, really stands out and grabs your attention. We can't get enough of everything, even those pretty rugs.

unique pieces. There are some plain white walls mixed in with darker shades and more earthy, lighter shades. The artwork on the walls is a great addition that goes great with the curtains, especially in the master bedroom.

The bedside lamps are very interesting pieces that sit on top of charming, well-designed bedside tables. They are both aesthetically pleasing and useful. The bed is made up of plain white sheets that have been decorated with Pendleton furniture to make it look better. You can't take your eyes off of that beautiful smile because the colors and pieces in the room go so well together.

Rooms for sleep

We'll now go to the private rooms. It will take a few years, but the building will eventually be the hub of the business. That's three rooms that are used as beds.

There is a half-vault in the roof of the 16x15 master bedroom. The girls' bedroom is the exact copy of the master bedroom in the other room. Baby's room is the room across from the master bedroom.

The rooms are just as well-designed as the rest of the house. The room is more than just a place to sleep thanks to its

The bathroom

Of course, people are still coming up with new ideas. You can find the same beautiful designs in the bathrooms of the Big Black Barn Oklahoma Barndominium as you can in the rest of the living space. This also applies to doors that are made just for you. The floating drawers give the bathroom a modern look. The saltillo tiles add a rustic feel to the room.

The mirrors are also made just for you and are very heavy. The story of how they "nearly burned the house down" while trying to hang these mirrors should be told. They accidentally drilled through wires, cutting off the power.

It took three or four days and a lot of different things to put this up. Well, these pretty things are well worth the work. Could also give us ideas; do whatever it takes to get the look you want!

Obsidian marble is used for the countertops, and sheepskin is used for the soft bath rugs. The bathroom should have a classic look with a western twist. The western look can be achieved with Pendleton towels and a fun western towel hook.

There is something a little different about the vaulting design in the shower, but it's still really cool. The shower tiles, on the other hand, look more classic and classy.

The Shed

The barn is downstairs. Four stalls, a wash rack, a tack room/office, a workshop with even more hanging storage, runoff stalls, a lean-to, and a porch are all there. The barn has big ceiling doors, and the stall gates look like the batwing doors upstairs. To get to the alley, there are Dutch doors. In the middle of the barn, there is a drive-through lane that is big enough for a full-sized truck and trailer.

You can still have fun making it feel a little cozy even though it's a barn. You can feel very at ease in the reading area and the sitting area in the barn.

Chapter 5

Cozy Converted Barn Barndominium with Loads of Style

A lot of barndominums are built to look like barns, even though they are meant to be houses. This might make you wonder if turning an old barn into a house is a good idea. You can decide for yourself if converting a barn is a good idea after seeing this cozy and stylish converted barn barndominium.

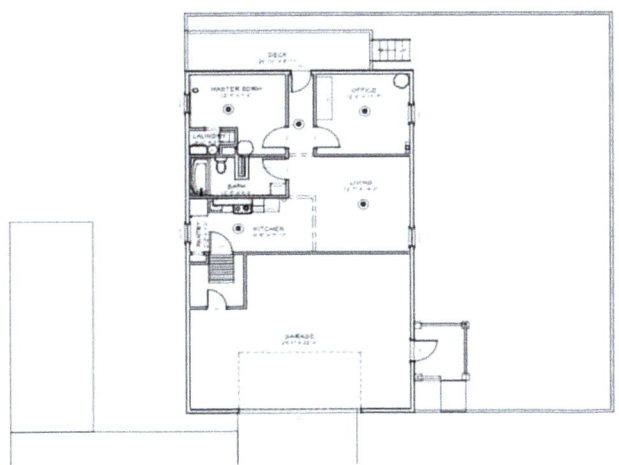

Outside and the garage

The outside of this barndominium still looks like a barn. It is a long, straight, rectangular building with a roof that slopes slowly down. One wall is taken up by a big garage door. The other walls have an entry door and a few windows each.

This barndominium still has a dull red color that makes it look like a barn. The outside of this barndominium has only been changed by adding a deck on the wall across from the garage door. There are many old trees around it, which gives the area a sense of timelessness.

With just a simple wooden wall between it and the rest of the house, the garage is very simple. It's big enough for two cars or a lot of tools, home items, and other things.

A door is the wall that separates two rooms and lets you get to the other parts of the house. Several wood cutouts of beer bottles, an overflowing mug, and old street signs make up the simple decoration. A few floating boxes hold other decorations and things that need to be stored.

Room for Living

The living room is very charming, with a suede couch that goes around the room, prints on the walls, and baskets all over the place for different household items. A beautiful, shiny hardwood floor looks great next to clean, soft gray walls that are almost white but not quite.

The owners like music, as shown by the guitars and records hanging on the walls. Ductwork that isn't covered is cleverly hidden behind a door. The soft gray walls go well with the silver ducts.

With lots of big, soft pillows and blankets, the simple single bed in the middle of the room can also be used as a couch during the day. A simple palm tree and some paper stars hanging from the ceiling help to bring the room together.

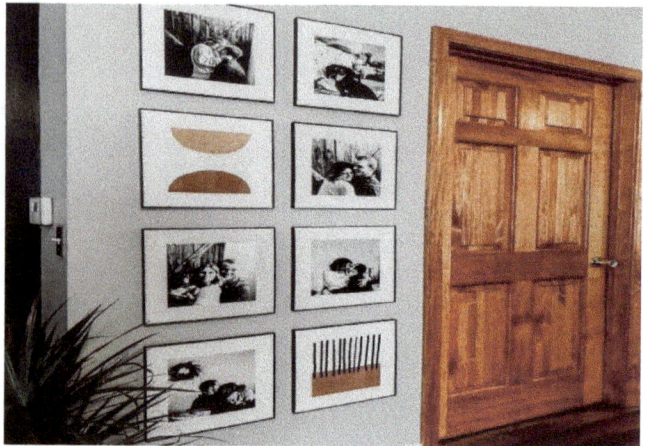

Office or guest room

The office and guestroom are very useful, with a desk and chair on one side and a big clothes rack out in the open on the other. Different kinds of papers and other junk are kept in wire boxes.

The brick accent wall and highly pigmented green walls on all four sides of this room make it look very stylish, even though it's a small, useful space. Both walls are colored by a big Persian area rug.

The window wall has corkboard panels connected to it, making it a great place to put different papers that need to be easy to get to. In this area, there are also some cute floating shelves and a dry-erase calendar in a frame with a clever design.

The kitchen and the dining room

The kitchen flows easily into the living room in this barndominium, which has an open floor plan. Sitting at the bar against one wall is a great way to eat breakfast quickly or do some light writing. It also helps make a wall between the living room and kitchen.

Another thing that helps separate them is that the floor goes from wood to tile. You can use this bar area as an extra surface in a kitchen that doesn't have a lot of counter room. The kitchen does look nice, though.

The light gray walls and ceilings look great with the almost black cabinets. Different glasses and other cooking items are stored on a bright red shelf above the sink and counter.

Behind the sink, a wall with waves that reflects light looks great in this room. The simple white tile countertops look nice and give the room a touch of modern-rustic style. The lack of closet space in this room means that there isn't much storage space without a built-in pantry.

There is a window in the living room and a window in the kitchen that are right next to each other. This lets natural light into both rooms.

The bedroom

The bedroom is very simple, with a simple metal bed frame that is open on all sides. Behind the headboard, an oval form has been painted as an accent to give this space more depth. The orange-and-copper blanket goes well with the shape of the headboard and takes ideas from the rest of the house.

A Persian rug under the bed also has this color in it. There are also blue details on the rug that match the throw pillows on the bed. This room has exposed ductwork that is tastefully covered. It goes across the room from the door to the other side of the room. The silver looks great with the light gray paint because it reflects light in a nice way.

Cozy Barndominum that was turned into a condo with lots of style

This cute house should give you ideas for what you could do with an old barn if you've ever thought about it. This is their first home, and they will love it for very many years. If you want more ideas on how to turn a barn into your own refuge, the Barndolife ebook is full of them.

Barndominium Interior Design Ideas

In the past few years, barndominiums have become very popular, and they are now a great choice for people who love the look of rustic country homes and rooms.

The features of each barndominium are different, and with some work, you can make it a place you love. A lot of people use these buildings as second homes. However, younger (and older) people are still interested in barndominiums, even though tiny homes and small-scale living have become popular in recent years.

Live out your house dreams

These 26 Barndominium decorating Ideas will give you some ideas for designing and decorating your home's interior.

1. **Simple Aesthetics**

Bring a sense of balance to your living space with barndominium living room ideas that show off the remodeled barn's rustic charm. The barn room is beautifully lit up by clean white stylistic elements.

The classic features mostly include simple design choices and materials that give the getaway a rustic feel. The dark wooden floors stand out against the bright white paint on the slat walls.

2. **Simple barn doors made of wood**

As part of design ideas for a barndominium, traditional wooden barn doors can be used to lead up to the living room. These are a great natural alternative to traditional French doors. They don't take up any extra room and let in lots of fresh air and light.

Add some simple black elements to make the outside look stylish. They add shape without making the all-white room look too busy.

3. **Bright and Diverse Personality**

One idea for a modern barndominium plan is to take a classic country barn and make it look more modern. Use white curtains and shiplap walls to keep the room light and open. The bright design is different from the cozy, simple colors that are usually found inside a barn. Wooden barn doors can give a room a beautifully simple feel.

4. **Used Barndominium Decor in New Ways**

As you look for ways to decorate a barndominium, try mixing furniture with both metal frames and natural materials. A wire basket can be turned into a wire shelf unit that you might see in farm-style decor.

A big, simple wall clock can be the center of attention in your room. Galvanized buckets can add a more rustic look, and elegant silver boxes look a lot like them. Green touches like plants can bring a place to life.

5. **Lofts in barns and metal ceilings**

Don't change the character of the traditional barndominium; instead, use the structure and architecture to make a place that is truly perfect. Because the ceilings were high, the wooden inside wouldn't look dark and squished.

With barn lofts, you can create a central place for conversation in a barndominium. The metal railing gives the classic wooden look a more rustic look. The old barn has a lot of empty room that can be used well in a modern barndominium.

6. **Inside of a barndominium kitchen**

A big kitchen is an important part of a barndominium home. To make your kitchen feel more like a country gathering place, add bar stools and butcher block countertops. You can give your bar stools a splash of color.

The rich wood tones that can be seen on the beams throughout the country home are reflected in the countertops. If your roof is vaulted, you might be able to add a barn loft that gives your kitchen more character and a vintage look.

7. **Charm of the Country**

Adding an open floor plan from the kitchen to the living room could make the barndominium cozier, warmer, and more stylish. People who own homes make good use of the open floors, which are usually found in barns, to divide up their space.

Along with the uncovered beams, white wooden boards on the walls of the beautiful barndominium might make it even more interesting. The windows let in a lot of natural light, and the high ceilings make the room feel airier and more open.

8. Pastel aqua colors with a new look

Add some ease to your barndominium's decor with light, muted blues that go well with cool colors. The blues and greens make it more interesting and give it a classic country home style look. A trunk and a wire basket can be used in new ways to add style and make them very useful for storage.

These kinds of wooden pieces are common in classic country homes. Putting some plants into your rustic room can make it feel more fresh and positive.

9. Peaceful splash of color

Even if you live in a traditional barndominium, the walls can still be colored. Wood panel walls are required, but you can change them a bit to give the room a more modern, calm, and peaceful feel. The beams fall below the roof, so the living room might feel a little squished. To make the room feel rich, bright, and airy, paint the beams and roof white.

10. Fireplace made of logs in Barndominium

A natural fireplace with a classic mantel will be the center of attention in your living room. The rustic style of the barndominium is helped by the fireplace, which can make the room cozier and more interesting. The bright colors on the walls and the windows let natural light into the room. Don't put too much decoration inside the room so that the other things in it stand out.

11. Make the Look bigger.

The family room and kitchen in large barn conversions both have an open floor plan. From the ceiling to the furniture, these kinds of rooms have a light-colored plan. The one-color plan makes the room feel bigger and more open. Farmhouse country kitchens have open shelves and cabinets made of glass that reflect light, which are typical of rural kitchens.

12. Barn has lots of rich, warm colors.

Adding the light-colored neutrals of the cushioned furniture goes well with the warm, rich colors of the throw blanket and the bright bar stools. Putting the glass shelves in front of the window makes the room look bigger. The barndominium has a lot of windows that let natural light and fresh air into the room.

13. The Look of the Lodge Design

A classic lodge style is used in barndominium decorating ideas to make a home that is cozy and comfy. A barn with different tones of wood is said to feel more open and have more depth. The floors, ceilings, beams, stairs, and cabinets in a barndominium are all made of wood.

This person wants to keep the design from being too busy, so they might paint the wood in different colors or use different types of wood.

14. A loft in a barndominium

Adding a country wall in the living room that already has wooden floor planks on it will give your barndominium an old-fashioned look. Building an archway from the living room to the bathroom and putting a traditional country fireplace in the middle of it will look great. The whole barndominium stays true to its theme of open movement, light, and simple design.

16. Bathroom floor made of wood

With the traditional barn loft that looks out over the kitchen's common area, you can make a classic, rustic sitting room. The lighter finish on the floor looks great with the darker kitchen table.

However, you don't have to get rid of the big barn features to make the space usable. In fact, they can give the space more character and depth. A modern touch can be added to a classic barndominium by hanging a pendant light from the ceiling.

15. Stone and wood features that look old

It's not true that you can't have a hard floor in your bathroom; it's just easier to keep clean. One way to do this is to seal the wooden floor with more coats of varnish. Put down a bath mat that soaks up a lot of water to protect the hard floor.

17. Double front doors on the barndominium

When designing the inside of these rustic rooms, barndominium double front doors are very popular. The way these doors meet in the middle to make a sunburst design gives the room a rustic feel. The wood used to make them is usually rough-hewn. Both the trellis and the barn doors have paneling that is an olive green color that goes well with the old wood.

18. Neutrals made of soft wood

The custom rustic barndominium design does a good job of showing off New England house decor. Let the soft gray color of the wooden furniture go well with the old, weathered wood. Instead of the warm orange tones that are common in barndominiums, you can choose to have your wooden floor a more mellow tone with a hint of gray.

Add a rustic feel to your barndominium with a fireplace that goes from the floor to the sky and has a wooden beam mantel.

19. Use hanging lights to light up the room.

The cathedral-style beams will help you match the long lines of your house. The vaulted ceilings of the standard barndominium are emphasized by these beams. Letting ceiling lights hang from the ceiling can add warmth, light, and charm to your home.

You can also choose a folding kitchen door, which will give your aged-style home a modern touch. Adding big windows will make the room feel lighter, cleaner, and more open. Add more wood to your living room by putting country furniture around it.

20. Raise your kitchen corner

If you want to take your classic kitchen's country style to the next level, choose a big table instead of a kitchen island. When shopping for a table, think about getting one with carved legs and an open bottom.

It can be very helpful to store wire baskets and copper pots that are both useful and pretty in the open area. To make a neutral color scheme more interesting, use dark to neutral color tones in your kitchen.

21. Describe the most basic traits

Steel frames and sheet metal are common parts of a classic barndominium. You can add a sheet metal roof to make it stand up to these factors. Beautiful white frame windows go well with the dark wood siding.

Keep things simple and straight to make the place look more sophisticated. The warm natural elements are wrapped around forms that are tailor-made and lines that are straight. To keep things raw and natural, put in a built-in corner shelf with the wood still on it.

22. Modern rustic furniture

To make the structure of the house look more interesting, use a rich design style that combines light colors with dark wooden beams. There are many beautiful hardwood floors that come in shades of red that you can add.

The gray paint on the double barn doors in the bedroom goes well with the white walls and paneling. The pendant lights give the room a touch of rich rustic luxury and a mix of styles.

23. Eco-friendly Barndominium

Making a long-lasting and eco-friendly house with traditional barn features and a barn loft with industrial steel wire railing is possible. You can make a spiral staircase that fits the room by designing it yourself.

Bring the industrial, raw look into the walls. An divider made from old steel roofing pieces can be used to separate the rooms. Having lush plants and trees inside will keep the air clean and bright.

24. Natural materials that are old

Embrace the natural beauty of things that are old and worn. Reclaimed wooden plank ceilings and long stone walls can be used together to make a cozy porch with windows.

A wooden plank floor painted in a lighter shade will help set the scene for a rustic classic barndominium without making the room too woody. Pillows with white leaf designs can add some pattern and a classy look to the room.

25. Organic and Rustic Elements

Learn how to decorate your barndominium with these tips. A field-stone half wall and a classic fireplace surround will give your barn a modern look. For the top, you might want to use an old beam that has been used for something else.

Put old things and gold highlights on top of the mantel, like an iron gate, dishes, and pots. A stone base and red-colored walls will give your barn a rustic look.

26. Architectural Salvage from a Barndominium

Peely and chipped building salvage can add a sense of age and texture to your living room. Use old, rusty sheet metal siding and window frames that have been chipped to add a rustic touch.

The rich barndominium living space will come to life with a big fireplace, a red wooden floor, and a cozy braided rug. Add industrial bar stools and a beautiful pendant light to finish off the room.

Barndominium Exterior Ideas You Will Love

If you want to buy a new house, you might want to think about building a barndominium. It's easy to see why barndominiums are becoming more and more popular. They have all the good things about regular homes, but they are a lot cheaper. On top of that, you can change them to fit your needs and tastes.

If you need some ideas, take a look at these beautiful barndominium exterior designs. They're great!

Beautiful exterior ideas for a barndominium that you will love

As the number of barndominiums built keeps going up, many builders are looking for unique exterior ideas to make their projects stand out. Here are some ideas for builders like them, or if you're just interested in what's popular right now.

If you are planning a new build or just starting to look into barndominiums, these beautiful outside designs are great to think about.

The best barndominium exterior ideas to think about

Having siding

You can choose from a lot of different siding types, and each has its own benefits. Adding some color or texture will make your home stand out, no matter what you choose. Instead, you might want to choose things that will still be in style in a few years. Some of these are:

- Aluminum exterior walls
- Putting up stucco
- Metals with ribs
- Vinyl Planks

Here are some great barndominium siding color choices that will make your home look better from the street:

- **White** is a classic color that makes things look softer.
- **Beige:** a great way to get a tan that doesn't look yellow. Even though not everyone likes beige, it is becoming more popular as a color for the outside of homes.
- **Bronze or brown:** This color looks great with a lot of shrubs and plants close to the house.
- **Dark gray** is a great color that goes well with any other color. You can pair dark gray with almost any color of trim.
- If dark gray isn't dark enough for you, black is a great choice. **Black** never goes out of style and never gets dirty.

It doesn't matter what color or texture of siding you pick as long as you love it. How your home looks on the outside will show how you feel on the inside.

Roof

When choosing a roof, you should think about how much it will cost, how easy it is to maintain, and the color options. Roofs come in shingles, clay tiles, and metal. A roof can improve the outside of a house. Painting and landscaping the outside of your home are great ways to make it look better from the street, but metal roofs make the whole thing feel old-fashioned. In a lot of colors, they can match any style or design, and they last a long time too. If you don't want to hear the noise that a metal roof makes, you might want to think about clay tiles.

One of the most common types of roof tiles in the world, clay tiles have been around for 5,000 years. You might have to pay more for clay tiles, but they will last longer than any other roofing material.

Take all the time you need to make sure you choose the best roof for your home thanks to good information.

Outside Kitchen

People can gather with their friends and family in the outdoor kitchen. You can grill fish on a summer night or roast chicken for a holiday party in the winter. Having your own built-in BBQ area makes it easy and fun to have people over.

When you plan your outdoor kitchen, think about how you will use the space and what you can see from your home. Make sure that the things you use and look at in it are things you will enjoy. Being able to cook outside is helpful, and I'm sure you'll be glad you spent the money to add one to your barndominium.

Landscape

What better way to improve the look of the outside of your home than to work on your landscaping? Your home will look better than ever if you plant some native trees and shrubs. Because landscaping can cost a lot, you don't have to do everything at once. Begin small and add to it over time.

Adding a pond to your property can make the natural beauty of your yard stand out even more. If you have a lot of land, you might want to add this on to your house. Building and maintaining a pond isn't too hard, and you and your family can enjoy it for years to come.

Columns

Your home's columns not only hold up the building, but they can also look great from the outside, especially if you add stonework to them and stain them to match any color scheme.

Patio

Is there a place outside your barndominium where you can relax? Then adding a patio to the outside of your barndominium is the right thing to do. You could even turn the patio into a covered porch that goes all the way around your house. If you want to put chairs and tables outside, this gives you a lot of room!

Lots of windows

Adding big windows to your home can help you enjoy the outdoors and make it look better. Plus, bigger windows let in more natural light, which makes any room feel bright, alive, and inviting!

The chimney

A brick chimney is one type, but there are also metal chimneys that look great. They're a great way to show off your personal style and tastes in your home! A chimney is a great thing to think about adding to your barndominium outdoor ideas.

In conclusion

You should think about adding at least one of these beautiful barndominium outdoor ideas to your new build if you want to make the outside look just the way you want it. You will love calling your new home yours no matter which one you pick from this list.

Spacious Tennessee Barndominium | 2600 Sq Ft Living Space and a Huge Garage with Glass Door

The outside of the Tennessee barndominium

The living room and even the garage can be really big, which is one of the best things about barndominiums like this Tennessee Barndominium that we picked out. Coming from the outside, this warm white and iron ore-colored outside makes us wonder what's inside. At first glance, the outside of this beautiful home looks almost black and white. Its simplicity belies its size.

For fun, a porch that goes all the way around the house is very useful. The outside looks even better because the Cypress wood used for the posts is its natural color. The entrance is lit up by an antler chandelier that matches the wood posts exactly. Barn lights keep the rest of the porch bright as well.

The black window and door trims look great against the white wall and match the color of the roof. The front windows are placed in an interesting way.

The Garage

The outside living area is very charming, but the drive-through 40x50 garage with ceilings as high as 14 feet is what you really need to see. Aside from being very big, what makes it interesting is that it has glass doors, which we haven't seen many barndos with. Making sure there is a lot of natural light inside without having to open the garage doors or the lights is a great idea.

need things like stainless steel tools, enough storage space, and a backsplash that matches the colors. The whole thing is warm white. Of course, the color of the rock in the middle is also very nice.

You will be amazed at how much space there is in this huge house when you walk into the barndo.

In front of the kitchen, there is a big veneer stacked stone fireplace with pretty white shiplap walls. The concrete floors are beautiful and look just like real wood floors. The stained pine wood roof that went across the whole mezzanine is a beautiful feature.

The roof of a barndo is 18 feet on the sides and 24 feet in the middle. This makes the inside light and airy, and the large glass doors and windows let you see the outside very well. Ceiling fans are also put up to make sure air moves freely inside.

Inside of a Tennessee barndominium

There are 3 bedrooms and 2.5 bathrooms in this large Summertown barndominium. As soon as the doors open, you look right into the kitchen. Also, if you're a friend, something must be cooking for you, so please come in. The kitchen isn't very big or fancy. In a small kitchen, you'll

Second Level

As you stand on the balcony, you can see the whole downstairs area, the big fireplace, and even more of the outside. The second floor is also very roomy, just like the first floor. On this floor, there are two bedrooms and a shared bathroom. You could also have another living room.

Rooms for sleep

The last bedroom is upstairs, and the master bedroom is on the first floor, in the hallway behind the kitchen. There is a beautiful pine ceiling, shiplap walls, and vinyl "wood" flooring in the master bedroom.

great. The chandelier in the middle of the bathroom and the black water fixtures make this bathroom look so classy. Plus, who can say no to a nice shower head? It's so cool to have in the shower!

The upstairs full bathroom is in the middle and can be reached from both beds. The bathroom also has two sinks, one at each end. When it comes to cleaning, the fact that the bathroom wall is more like fiberglass and acrylic than tile is very helpful. This is very important since kids use the bathroom together.

Bathrooms

Walls and ceiling made of shiplap match those in the master bedroom in the bathroom. The bathroom has a big tub and two sinks. The ceramic tile wall in the shower room looks

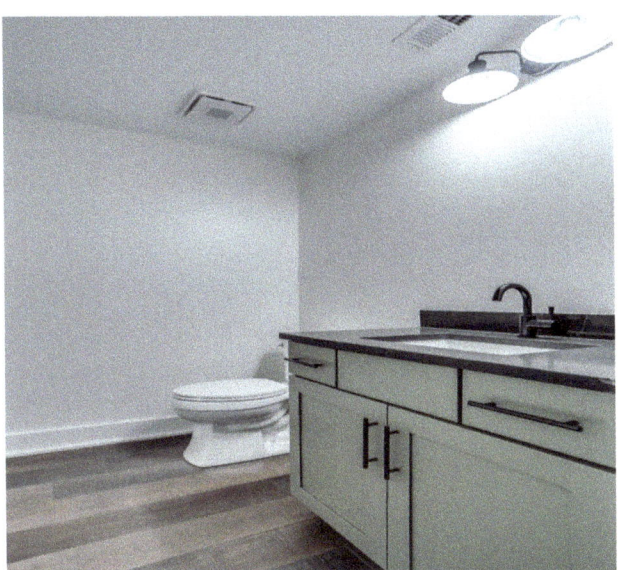

The Long and Short of It...

Sometimes it's hard to build the barndominium of your dreams. Along the way, you will have problems and get angry. You need to be brave, determined, and guided to make it happen, especially if you don't want to make any mistakes.

It is well worth the money to buy a barndominium for your family in the long run.

Chapter 6

Mistakes to Avoid When Building Your Barndominium

If you plan to construct your own Barndominium, you are undoubtedly aware of the advantages and disadvantages of these special buildings. Even with its simplicity, building a Barndominium still involves a lot of considerations.

Here are the top 12 mistakes to avoid while creating your Barndominium so that it lasts for many years:

1. **Not Calculating Your Budget Before Beginning Construction**

It might be annoying to run out of money in the middle of a project, particularly if you don't have any other sources of funding. You are left with an unfinished house that is unfit for occupancy.

Have a firm understanding of your finances before beginning construction to make sure you have enough money to cover the cost of your full Barndominium.

2. **Monitoring Site Operations Prior to Building**

Buildings, including barndominiums, are constructed on foundations. It is necessary to carefully prepare the land before laying the foundation; never underestimate the significance of leveling and making sure the earth can support the foundation and the structure.

3. **Not Planning for Upgrades**

Handy kits are available for barndominiums. These kits, however, come with a predetermined quantity of doors, windows, and other parts. You will need to order additional materials if you wish to install more windows and doors.

This raises the total cost of creating your Barndominium; keep these facts in mind when figuring out how much it will cost.

4. **Making Your Own Drawings of the Floor Plan**

There is more design and layout versatility when building your own Barndominium.

The floor can be adjusted to your preference. You can create the floor plan yourself, but since there are other crucial considerations, it is imperative that you collaborate with a professional constructor. They consist of things like natural lighting, warmth, cooling, and structural support. Living space depends critically on the dimensions and layout of each room as well as the corridor.

5. **Unwise Land Selection for Your Barndominium**

Unless you already own the land on which you plan to build your barndominium, you might have to hunt for a suitable residential neighborhood with less restrictive building codes.

For instance, Wisconsin barndominium ideas work better in rural than in urban settings. Considerations for building a Barndominium include road access, security, ease of access to services, property size, neighboring properties, and more.

6. Choosing the Incorrect Contractor

A competent builder can aid in streamlining the overall building procedure. Hiring experts has the benefit of assisting you in avoiding errors and saving money.

Some contractors see projects with self-serving motivations, even if the majority of them are trustworthy and sincere. Selecting the incorrect contractor may cause project delays and higher expenses.

7. Underestimating Your Barndominium's Height

A two-story Barndominium, for instance, is higher and provides more capacity for additional rooms. Certain local governments have height limitations on structures within their jurisdictions.

A lower roof pitch can be necessary for a higher Barndominium, depending on the constraints. The height that can be used for additional levels is greatly influenced by the frames of these buildings. If you want a two-story Barndominium, make sure the frame size and available space will allow it.

8. not designating a deadline for completion.

Whether you hire an expert contractor or do it yourself, you must set a rough completion date for your Barndominium construction.

Your project may take longer to complete without one, which would raise the cost of construction. Establish a deadline and collaborate with the expert you hired to meet it.

9. Insufficient Wall and Roof Insulation

The majority of barndominium construction uses steel frames and metal sidewalls. In the summer, these materials absorb heat; in the cold, they lose heat. You must adequately insulate in order to maintain a pleasant room temperature throughout the cold months.

10. Not Verifying Your Community's Building Codes

various places have various building codes, therefore it's important to verify with the local government. Getting permission to build your Barndominium can be necessary. You don't want to make the mistake of neglecting to check or disobeying the construction codes in your area as it could result in expensive fines.

11. Neglecting to Include Overhangs on Big Windows and Doors

Rainwater is largely diverted away from your Barndominium's foundation by eaves and gutters. Regretfully, they don't offer your property enough protection.

Rainwater might result in flooding and pooling around your Barndominium frame unless it is constructed on an elevated foundation. Soil erosion occurs over time and weakens your foundation. To safeguard your property, think about installing an overhang on wide windows and doorways.

12. Managing Everything on Your Own

Constructing a Barndominium is a substantial do-it-yourself undertaking. It is advised that you engage with a professional unless you have sufficient experience managing large-scale initiatives. If certain tasks are not performed by experts, they might easily go wrong during construction.

A series of small errors might eventually cause larger issues. Qualified personnel are needed for tasks like plumbing and electrical installations. Should you attempt to handle things on your own, you will face a variety of difficulties.

In summary

Without a question, building a barndominium is typically quicker and easier than building a regular home. They come in kits that make building them easier and are much more robust.

After reading this book, you should be aware of the top 12 mistakes to make when creating your Barndominium. You can save money and save building time by avoiding several blunders.

Building a Barndominium in Colorado

One of the hardest things you will ever do is build your own house. In the long term, nevertheless, it might also be among the most fruitful. Not everyone has the opportunity to design a house that is constructed to their exact specifications, but for those who can, the time and effort required can be well worth it. But if you've ever researched the process of building your own house, you are aware of the amount of work and effort involved. It can also be very costly, which prevents many individuals from being able to afford it.

For this reason, constructing a barndominium in Colorado can be a really wise choice. You may construct the house of your dreams without having to go through all the hoops you would typically have to because it is less expensive and easier to construct. With the rise of the alternative housing movement, barndominium sales are increasing, and more banks and builders are beginning to enter the market. As a result, it is more than ever the perfect time to consider constructing a barndominium in Colorado.

Everything you might possibly want to know about constructing a barndominium in Colorado is included in this book. You may build the house of your dreams lot more easily than in the past if you follow these guidelines and make sure everything is planned properly.

What Are Some Benefits of a Barndominium and What Is It?

A barndominium is a house constructed on the framework of a metal post-frame building or pole barn. Typically, these types of structures are utilized for commercial or agricultural purposes, such as stables or storage, but they may also be employed to construct stunning residences that you can personalize to your exact needs. You would never even be able to tell that the house was constructed with non-traditional materials if you framed them up inside like you would with a regular home.

The fact that creating a barndominium in Colorado can be significantly less expensive than building a traditional home is one of its key advantages. A barndominium rises from the ground almost half as quickly as a typical dwelling. This is because the buildings are simpler to frame up by driving the poles into the ground and cement-securing them, as well as the concrete slab base. The simplicity of building allows you to save a significant amount of money on materials and labor.

Durability is another benefit of constructing a barndominium in Colorado. Steel siding and posts, used in the construction of barndominiums, are resistant to decay, mildew, and mold. These items could be an issue in a conventional home in a place like Colorado where snowfall is common. Nevertheless, over time, you may save money on repairs if you use a barndo.

Colorado Barndominium Construction Cost

After deciding to construct a barndominium in Colorado, you should consider your financial situation. Finding your construction's cost per square foot is the easiest way to do this. You will be able to determine how big your concrete slab foundation should be and how much house you can afford by doing this, which is one of the benefits. You can then choose the number of bedrooms and bathrooms you want and where you want them located in the house.

In Colorado, the price of constructing a conventional home is about $136 per square foot. It's crucial to remember that this amount just covers the building's initial construction. It does not cover items like finishing or furniture, which you will need to purchase separately with additional funds from your budget. This can drive up the price of your purchase beyond your means.

In Colorado, the cost of creating a barndominium is significantly less. In Colorado, the average cost to build a barndominium is $108 per square foot. You might be able to get everything you could ever want in a custom-built home with the money you saved. With this extra cash in the budget, items like furnishings, electronics, even cabinetry and countertops might all be purchased.

Colorado Barndominium Builders

You will need to consider who you will engage to complete the constructing once you have established a budget for your Colorado barndominium. Your barndominium project may succeed or fail depending on the builder you choose, but if you can work with someone who truly cares about your needs, you will be able to feel secure during the whole undertaking. However, there are a lot of different types of builders in the construction industry, so it might be challenging to choose the ideal one for your project. Fortunately, there are a few indicators you can look out for to determine whether or not you're making the appropriate choice.

Experience with metal post frame buildings is the first quality a builder in Colorado should have when starting a barndominium project. It is crucial that you locate a builder with prior experience building this kind of structure, since not all builders will possess the necessary skills for this particular project. The procedure is distinct, and doing it right requires expertise. Seek for a builder with experience in this kind of work, if you can.

Additionally, you want to search for a builder with a solid customer service record. It's important that you get along with your builder, and you should make sure they can provide the kind of experience you require to feel at ease. We've compiled a list of some of Colorado's top barndominium builders to help you get started on your search and pick the one that's right for you.

Drop Tine Construction

Although Drop Tine Construction has only been in operation since 2016, all of its builders have prior experience in building and construction, which supports the company's mission. They are an excellent option for constructing a barndominium in Colorado because they are rooted in the neighborhood.

Sunset Buildings

Nearly all of Sunset Buildings' clientele consists of recurring business. This indicates that they have the ability to provide their clients with high-quality products and customer service, and it is quite probable that they will be able to provide you with the same.

Pregio Houses

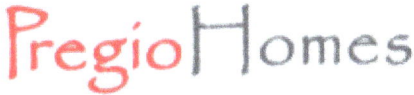

Pregio Homes is proficient and experienced due to their commitment to the barndominium construction process in Colorado. They can swiftly and simply deliver a building that is precisely constructed to your needs because their entire business is centered around their building method.

Colorado Barndominium Kit Providers

There are alternatives available to you if you don't want to construct your Colorado barndominium from the ground up, such a barndominium kit. When the prefabricated barndominium kits arrive at your construction site, they are already fully assembled. They are therefore a fantastic choice if you don't want to take your time finding the supplies for your build.

The suppliers of Barndominium kits will assist you all the way through the building procedure. In fact, several of them even offer referrals for builders who have previously completed their kits. This implies that regardless of the stage of the build you are at, you will always have the assistance you require.

Colorado Barndominium Financing

Banks for Communities in Colorado

In order to locate the ideal loan for your specific needs, Community Banks of Colorado takes the time to get to know you and your goals. They have a really significant connection and are highly community-focused. They might be a fantastic option if you wish to operate with a bank that is willing to assist you.

Southern Colorado Farm Credit

Loans are available from Farm Credit of Southern Colorado for a variety of projects, including your Colorado barndominium. Together, you will determine the ideal terms for your project as well as your requirements for the duration and interest rate of the loan.

Colorado Barndominium Taxes

You will have to pay property taxes on your Colorado barndominium, just as you would on any other type of property. Nonetheless, the IRS considers certain barndominiums to be dual-use construction. This implies that different parts of your property, such as the residential and storage spaces, will be subject to separate tax rates. To determine the amount of taxes you should be paying, consult a local tax assessor.

Where in Colorado to Find Insurance for Barndominiums?

It is always a good idea to have insurance for your home, no matter what type it is. Your barndominium in Colorado will be no exception. You should constantly make sure that your barndominium is covered for any emergency. Sometimes, this implies that you will need to have additional clauses with your policy to cover things like wildfire or flooding. Check with your local insurance agent to find out how you should be covered.

Barndominium Floor Plans in Colorado

The floor plan is one of the most crucial things you will put together for your barndominium in Colorado. The floor plan spells out how everything in the home will be arranged including bedrooms, bathrooms, and living areas. To get started, put together a list of everything you want to include in your floor design. Then, take that list to a competent draftsman. They will utilize it to develop a functional floor design that you and your contractor can use to build your barndominium in Colorado.

In summary

You ought to have a solid understanding of the requirements for constructing a barndominium in Colorado after reading this article. You may expedite the project by being aware of what to expect at each stage and what you should be doing in advance.

Chapter 7

Modern Farmhouse Plans with Barndominium Style

Searching for a place to call home in the country? Check out these modern farmhouse plans with a barndominium style (mainly typical wood framing, while the term barndominium often refers to a metal construction). Large kitchens, board-and-batten siding, and inviting porches all convey a classic yet contemporary vibe. These are eleven striking illustrations.

Style Barndo with Enclosed Porch

Wraparound Porch in Barndo Style (1064-111) - Front Exterior

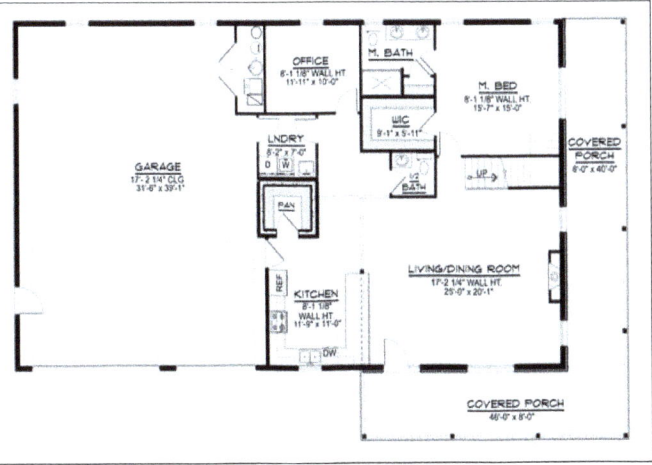

Barndo Style Main Floor Plan 1064-111 with Wraparound Porch

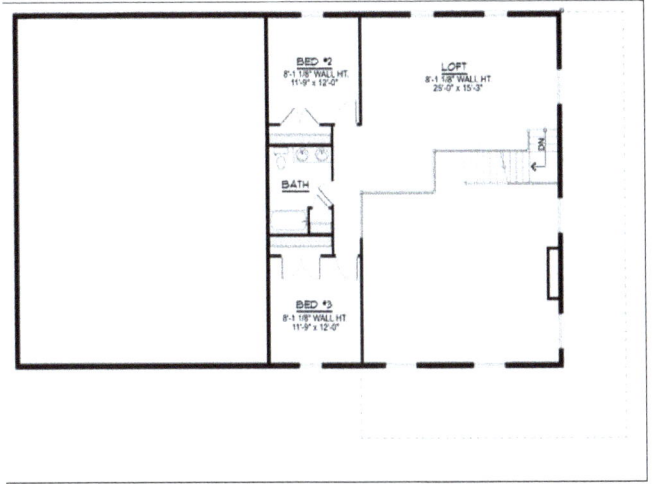

Wraparound Porch in Barndo Style (1064-111) - Upper Floor Plan

This is a contemporary farmhouse design in the barndo style. The aluminum gable roof and the stylish wraparound porch are our favorites. The interior design has an open floor plan connecting the main living rooms, giving the space a calm and airy sense. Take a look at the large garage and the home office.

For ease of aging in place, the main suite is located on the main floor. A complete bathroom is shared by two secondary bedrooms above. Don't overlook the adaptable loft.

Carport with Three Cars and Workshop

Workshop 1064-148 - Front Exterior Three-Car Garage

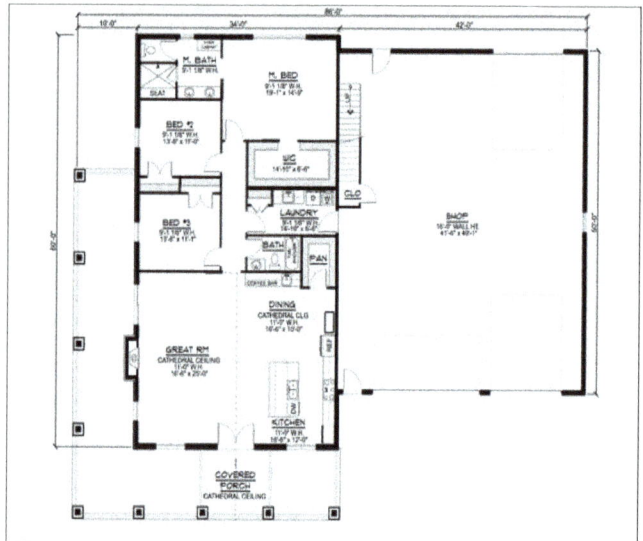

Main Floor Plan for a Three-Car Garage with Workshop 1064-148

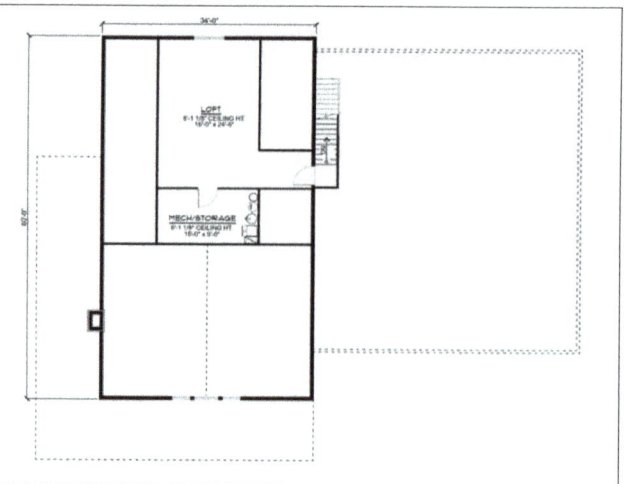

Upper Floor Plan for a Three-Car Garage with Workshop 1064-148

This modern farmhouse style has a wraparound porch that greatly enhances its curb appeal. Note the spacious three-car garage and workshop as well; these are lovely barndominium features. The large kitchen island looks out over the living area, making you want to unwind.

The main suite's roomy walk-in closet makes it simple to maintain clothing organization. Completing the second floor are a storage area and an adjustable loft.

Generous Kitchen Island

Massive Kitchen Island 932-521 - Front Outside

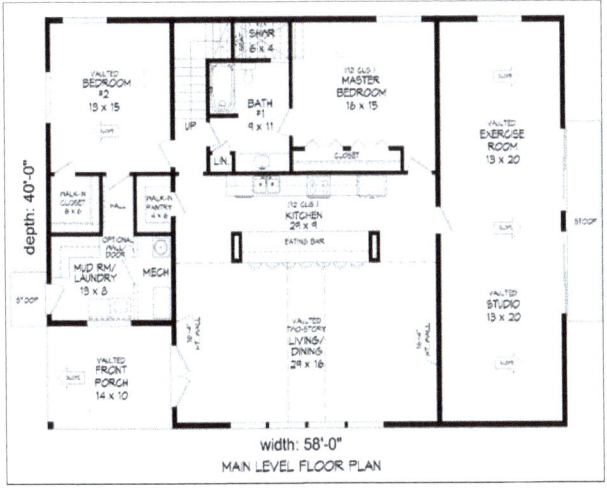

Large Kitchen Island - Main Floor Plan 932-521

Front exterior of a modest farm house (124-1263).

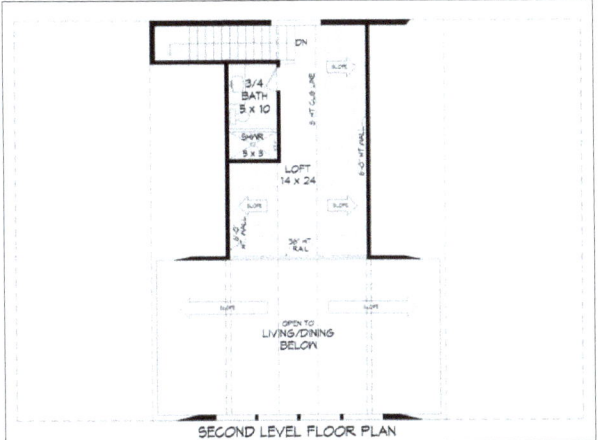

Large Kitchen Island - Upper Floor Plan 932-521

View this plan for a barndominium house. Opening to the dining space and living room is an amazing kitchen island with seating for seven, complete with an eating bar. You'll value the adjoining spacious mudroom/laundry area and the handy walk-in pantry.

Nice extras include a studio area and a lofty fitness room. There is a shower-equipped bathroom and a loft on the upper floor.

Simple Farmhouse

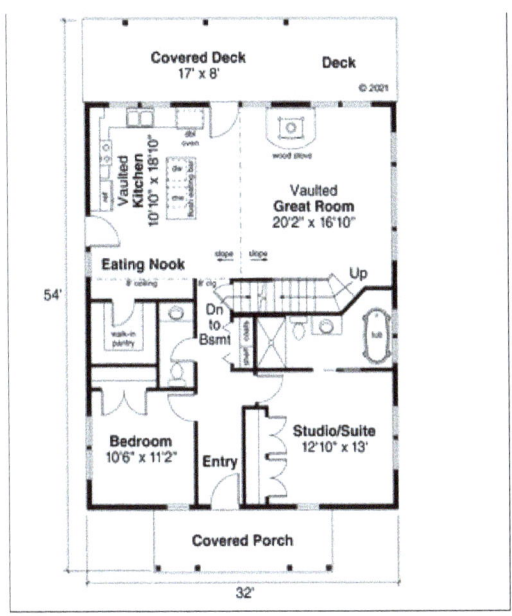

Main Floor Plan of the Modest Farmhouse 124-1263

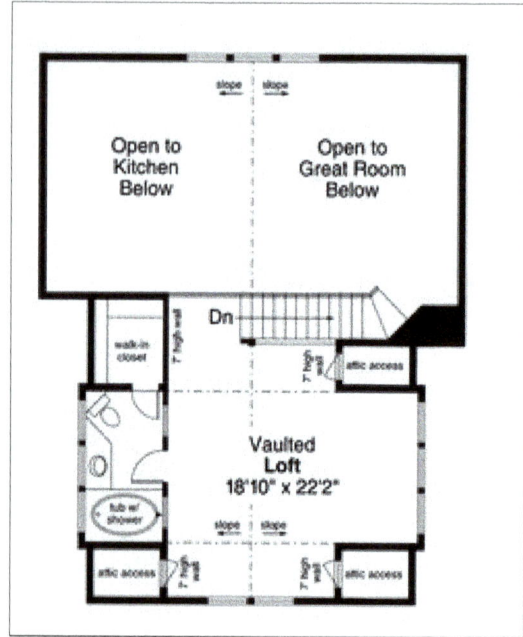

Simple Farmhouse 124-1263: First Floor Layout

This charming country home combines a contemporary floor plan with traditional farmhouse features like board-and-batten siding, a gable roof, and a welcoming front porch. The big room has a wood stove and a high ceiling. A central island, a flush dining bar, and a walk-in pantry with shelving are features of a well-equipped kitchen.

Completing the main floor are an additional bedroom and the main suite. Versatility is increased upstairs with a loft and a complete bathroom.

Greeting Spirit

Friendly Atmosphere 430-259 - Front Exterior

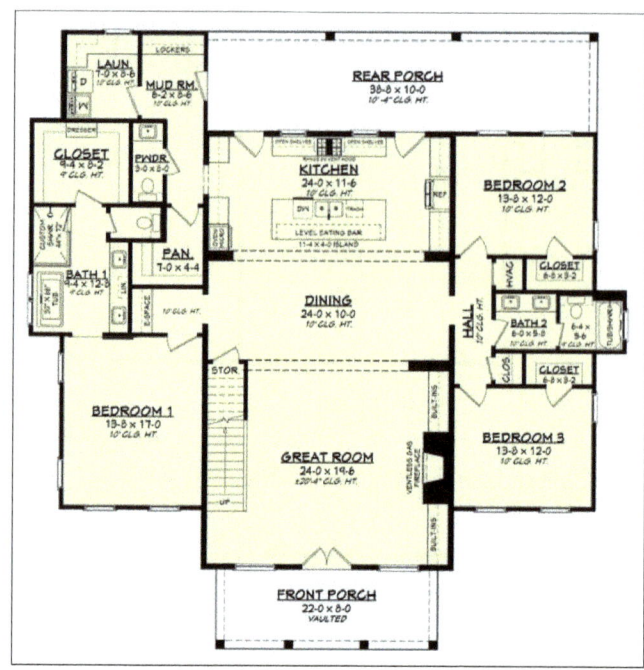

Warm Ambience 430-259 - Main Floor Layout

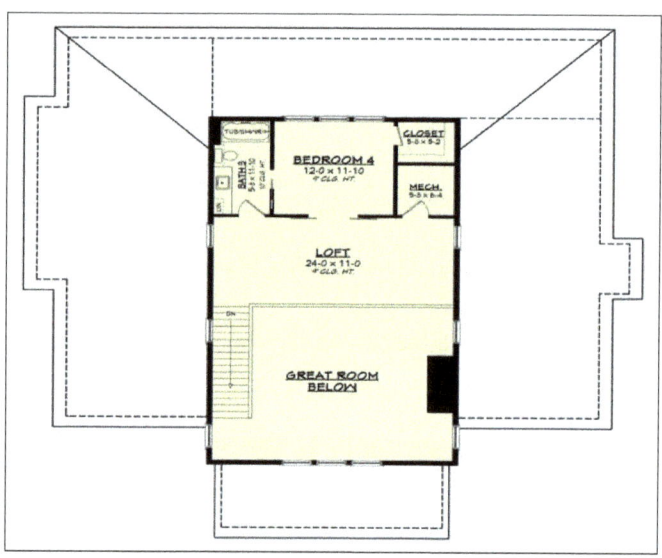

Warm Ambience 430-259 - First Floor Layout

This contemporary farmhouse design boasts a charming front porch and gorgeous board-and-batten siding for a rustic curb appeal. The dining area and great room are accessible from the kitchen thanks to the functional layout. There's room for everything in the spacious pantry.

The main suite has plenty of seclusion thanks to the split-bedroom layout. A convenient loft, a large back patio, and walk-in closets in every bedroom are further features.

Effective Floor Design

Optimal Floor Plan 120-274 - Exterior Front

Main Floor Plan 120-274: An Effective Floor Plan

This farmhouse design showcases the metal-framed barndominium style. There is plenty of counter space in the country kitchen, which easily transitions into the family area. The main suite, which is tucked away toward the back of the layout, has a large walk-in closet, two sinks, and a safe room in addition to seclusion.

Near the front of the house, each of the two secondary bedrooms has a walk-in closet. A study adjacent to the entrance provides a peaceful workspace. Our favorite area is the large covered patio in back.

Easy Living Outside

Simple Outdoor Living - Front Exterior 1074-24

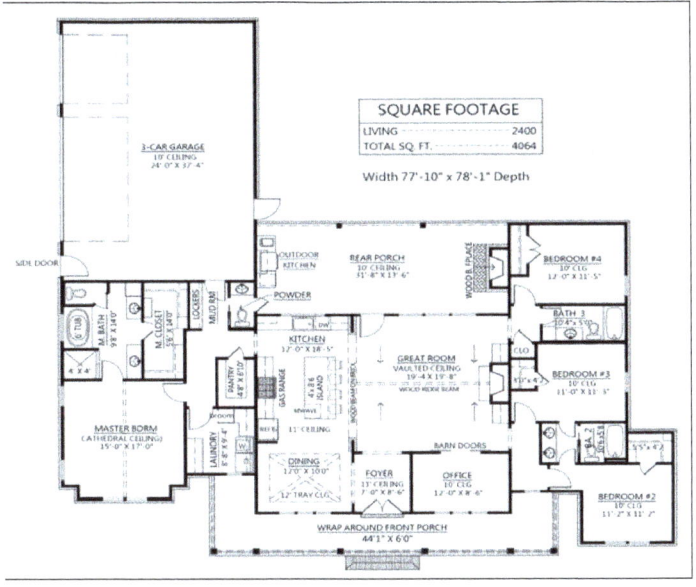

Main Floor Plan: 1074-24 - Easy Outdoor Living

This farmhouse is distinguished by its gable roof and classic wraparound porch. The contemporary interior design is both stylish and practical. The island kitchen in the main living rooms extends fully to the dining area and the great room. The main suite has a large walk-in closet and a spa-like bathroom.

The sophisticated drop zone with lockers by the three-car garage is a must-see. With barn doors, the home office offers solitude in a stylish manner. pleasant weather? Enjoy outdoor living to the fullest on the back porch, which has a wood-burning fireplace and a kitchen.

Small-Lot Farmhouse Design

Front Exterior of Narrow-Lot Farmhouse Plan 430-282

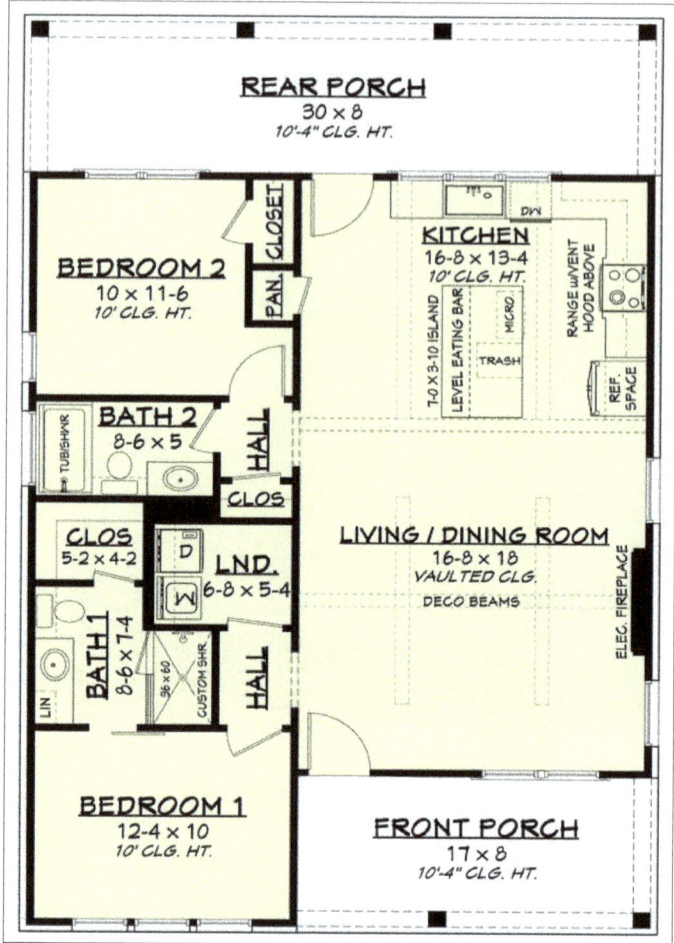

Main Floor Plan for Narrow-Lot Farmhouse Plan 430-282

This clever farmhouse plan, with its open form and efficient use of square footage, is perfect for a tiny lot. The dining/living room is easily served by the level eating bar in the kitchen. There are more outside living possibilities with front and back porches.

This layout is completed with the main suite, an extra bedroom, and a full bathroom.

Airy and Contemporary

Easygoing and Contemporary 1074-44 - Front Exterior

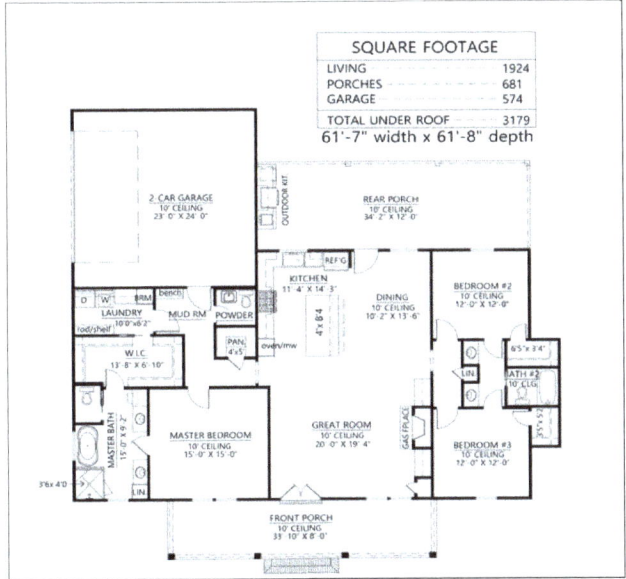

Airy and Contemporary - Main Floor Plan 1074-44

This farmhouse design is a true reflection of contemporary living. With an island, the kitchen is open to the great space. The house is shaded by covered porches on the front and back. Direct entrance to the washing room is provided by the main suite, which is located on the left side of the layout.

There are two further bedrooms with walk-in closets and a shared full bathroom on the other side. There's a seat added in the mudroom where you may remove your shoes.

Two-Level Farmhouse Plans

Front Exterior of a Two-Story Farmhouse Design 923-273

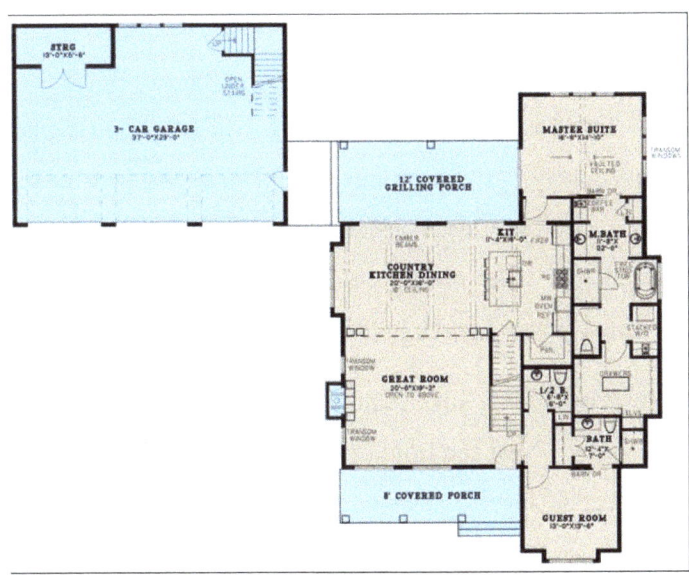

Main Floor Plan of a Two-Story Farmhouse Design 923-273

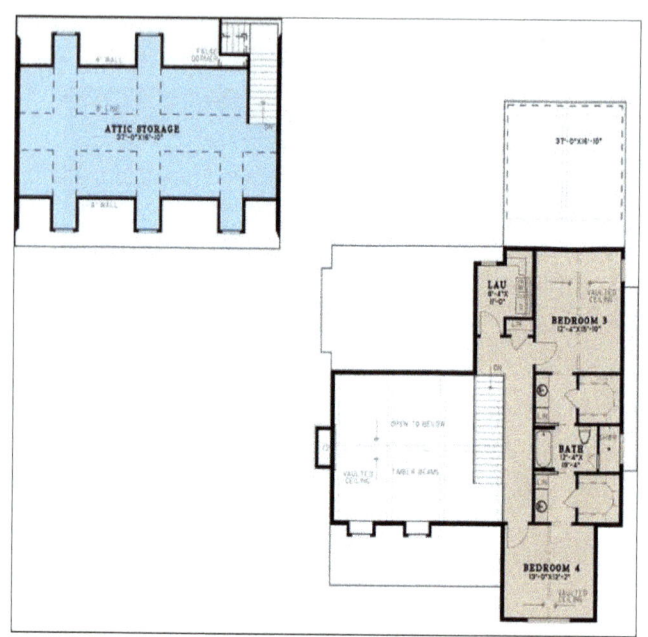

Lots of Storage - Front Exterior 51-1213

Design 923-273: Two-Storey Farmhouse with Upper Floor Plan

The farmhouse-style facade of this two-story house plan immediately draws your attention. The atmosphere inside is open and carefree. Look at the kitchen, which has a large island that seats people casually. Doors that slide open reveal a covered porch in back.

The private main suite features opulent features, such as a coffee bar! Near the front of the layout is a guest suite. On the second level, a Jack-and-Jill bathroom connects two bedrooms.

Lots of Storage Space

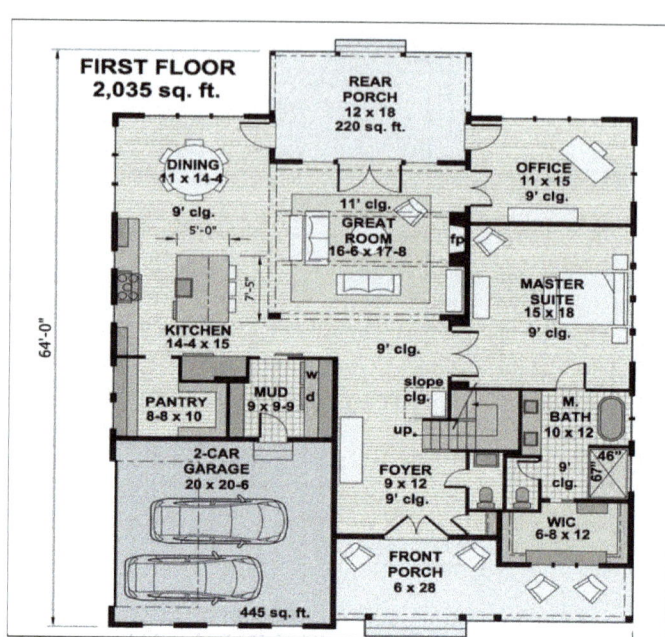

Lots of Storage - Main Floor Plan 51-1213

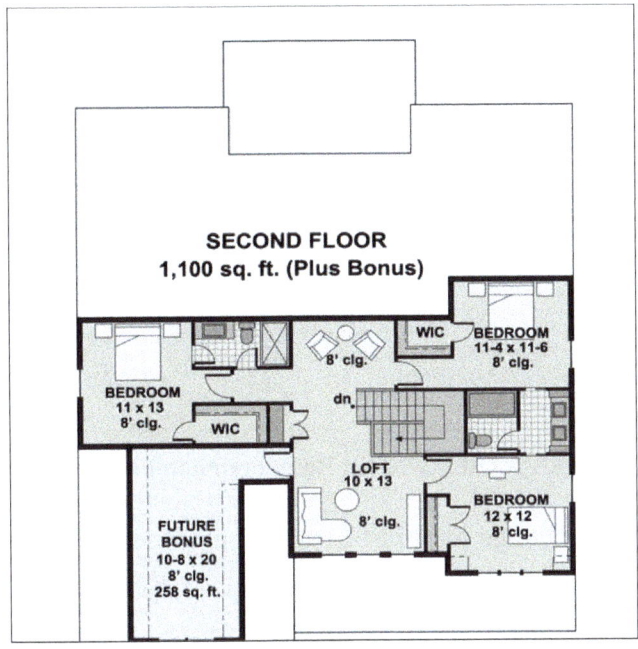

Recently, plans created by barndominium designers have become increasingly imaginative. One of the year's most fascinating and diverse design categories is the modern barndominium, which offers a variety of floor plans, including intimate cottages and large open floor plans with trendy amenities.

Choosing from the many features and specifications available in this design area could be challenging. Fortunately, we would be happy to share with you the barndominium floor plans that we already adore.

Small-scale Barndominium Floor Design

Lots of Storage (Upstairs Floor Plan 51-1213)

This four-bedroom farmhouse layout welcomes you with a broad front porch. The open kitchen and great room, with an island that makes it simple to serve meals here and to the dining area, are the focal points of this stunning plan. Practical storage is added by the walk-in pantry and mudroom.

Don't miss the amazing bathroom in the main suite, which features an extra-large closet and a soothing tub. Near the back of the layout, an office has access to the back porch. The second floor is completed with two bathrooms, a loft, and three more bedrooms.

Barndominium Floor Plans

Barndominiums, which are renowned for, well, looking like barns, have attracted a lot of attention in recent years.

Although most people associate the term "barndominium" with metal constructions, we describe barndominiums as any kind of structure that adheres to the barn aesthetic. This broadens the category to encompass floor plans with wood frames that have the rustic appearance of pole barn designs.

Simple Floor Plan for a Barndominium - Front Exterior

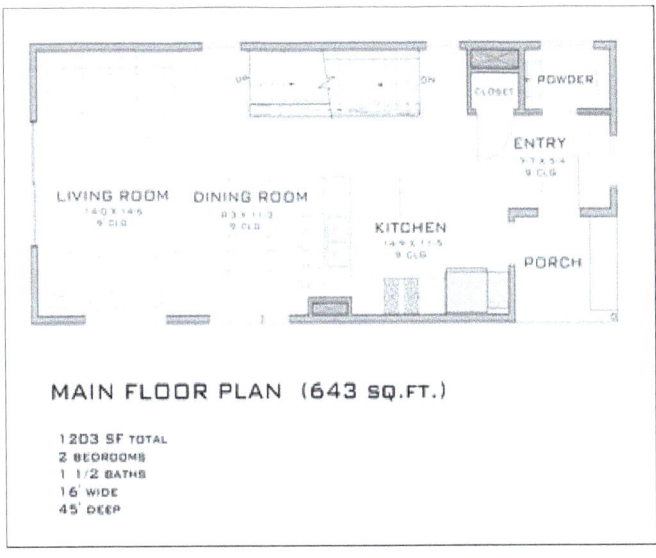

Main Floor Plan of a Modest Barndominium

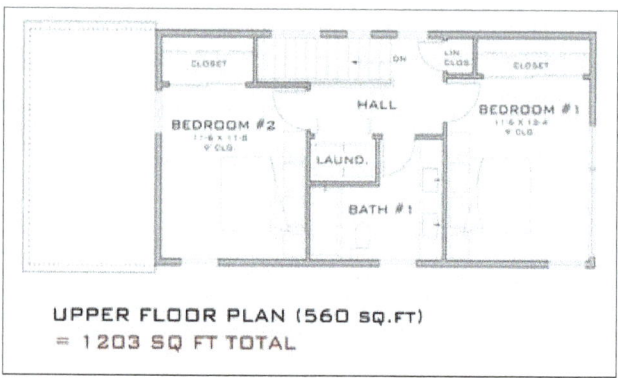

Floor Plan for a Modest Barndominium - Upper Level

Would you like to reduce room but still like the design of a basic barndominium? It is possible to fit this compact two-story, three-level layout onto almost any urban land.

This floor plan of a barndominium is distinctive because of how well the living and sleeping sections are divided. This design is easily customizable to meet a wide range of lifestyles, with the bedrooms situated on the upper and foundation levels and the living area situated on the main floor.

Plan of a Modern Barndominium

The front outside of a contemporary barndominium floor plan

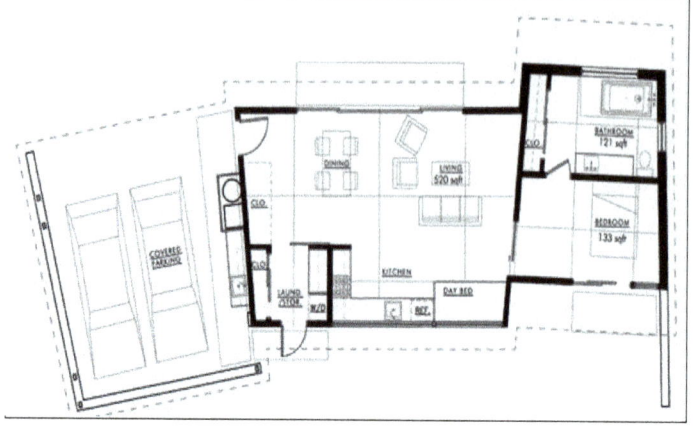

Main Floor Plan of a Modern Barndominium Floor Plan

This floor design for a rustic barndominium seems like it belongs in a Western film. It's a great weekend getaway home because of its open floor plan and slanted extended roof, which are great for staying cool during the summer heat. Even though the outside is straightforward and unpretentious, the interior will definitely wow.

Begone, little cottage bedrooms! With its spacious main bedroom suite and open living-dining area, this design offers plenty of space for relaxing without feeling crowded. This barndominium floor plan is ideal for anyone seeking more connection to nature, as it features an abundance of stunning windows and sliding doors that open up to the outdoors.

Examine this floor layout closely to identify our favorite feature. A well-positioned daybed just off the kitchen makes the ideal spot for unwinding after a weekend of overindulging in food.

Floor Plan of a Barndominium with Covered Porch

Front exterior of a barndominium floor plan with covered porch

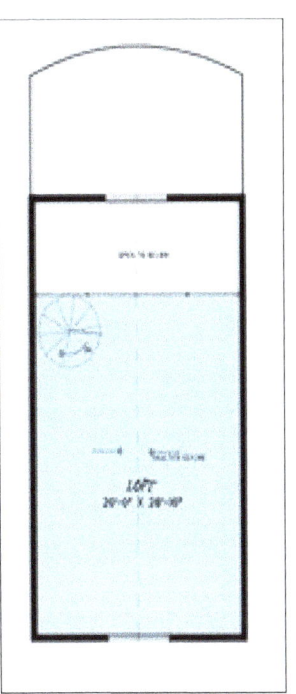

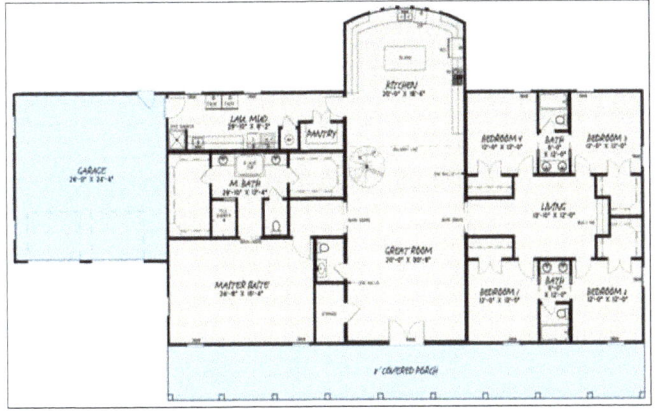

Main Floor Plan for a Barndominium with Covered Porch

Upper Floor Plan for a Barndominium with Covered Porch

Meet a floor plan for a barndominium that knows how to make the most of a big lot. totaling 3,277 square feet. This 5,500-square-foot, 3.5-bathroom layout is ideal for someone who likes the style of barndominiums but wants to add some luxury. A mudroom and an ensuite bathroom off the main bedroom with two walk-in closets are thoughtful amenities.

There is plenty of area in the large great room for dining, entertaining, and relaxing. For guests or older children, there is additional space and solitude thanks to the four additional neighboring bedrooms and separate living area in the middle.

There won't be a problem with counter space in the kitchen, but you might be too preoccupied taking in the view from that stunning bow window to spend time preparing meals (that's why there's delivery).

Plan of a Tiny Barndominium Floor

Floor Plan of the Tiny Barndominium - Front Exterior

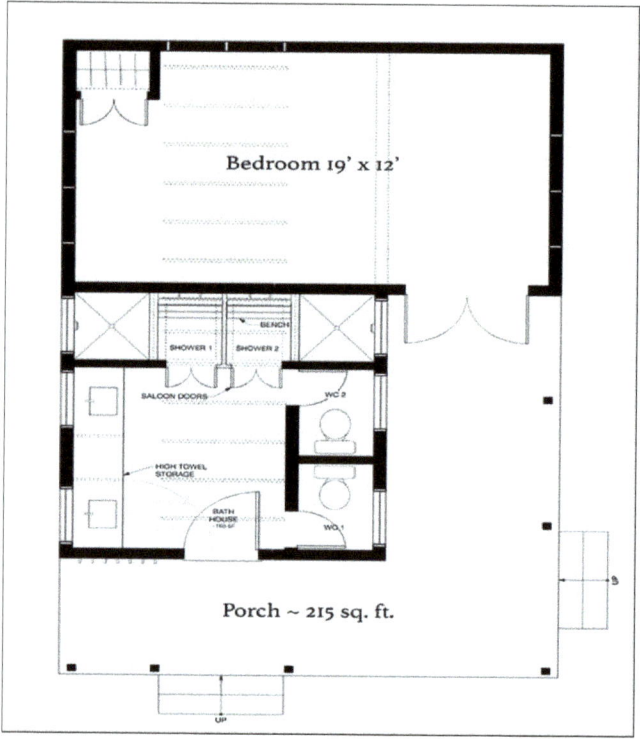

Main Floor Plan of the Tiny Barndominium Floor Plan

This little floor plan in the shape of a barn would be a great multipurpose addition to any backyard. Use it for outdoor activities as a bunkie, guest house, or pool house. With this one, the options are genuinely unlimited.

Describe a bunkie. Go here to read more from House Beautiful.

This charming and useful floor design fits a lot of functionality into a small 388 square feet. feet. With two bathrooms with walk-in showers, a spacious bedroom, and a kitchenette, this layout offers all the conveniences needed for a comfortable stay.

Floor Plan of a Barndominium with Workshop

Floor Plan of a Barndominium with Workshop - Front Exterior

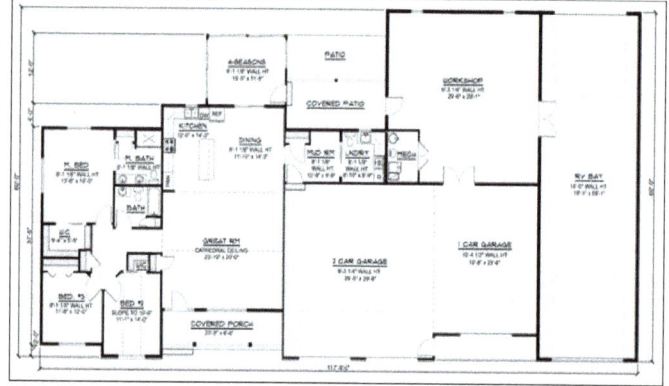

Main Floor Plan of the Barndominium with Workshop

This is an all-inclusive floor plan for a barndominium. Really, no.

This design, which includes two garages, an RV berth, and a workshop, is ideal for any auto fanatic. The bedrooms, great room, and living room are on the other end of the house, so family members won't have to worry about hearing any noise from the workshop area. You can be as sloppy as you like since there will be no trouble cleaning up after a demanding workday because there is a mud room and an adjacent laundry room.

Do you need a little fresh air? Not an issue. There are two covered outdoor spaces in this floor plan: one in the front and one at the back. You can enjoy the outdoors in any weather thanks to the magnificent rear patio that leads to an all-season lanai.

Floor Plan of a Barndominium with a Loft

Front exterior floor plan of a barndominium with a loft

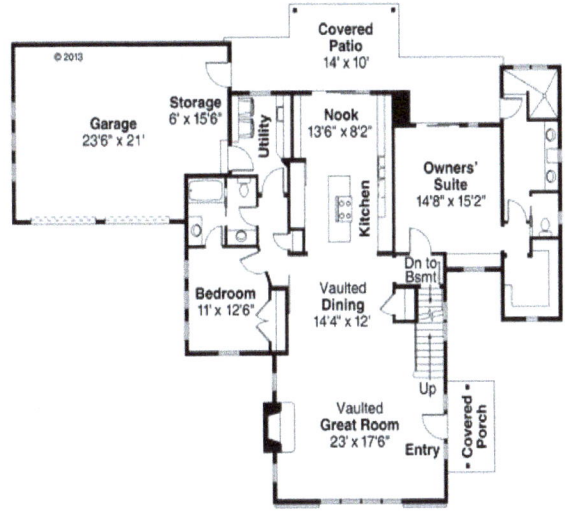

Main Floor Plan for a Barndominium with Loft

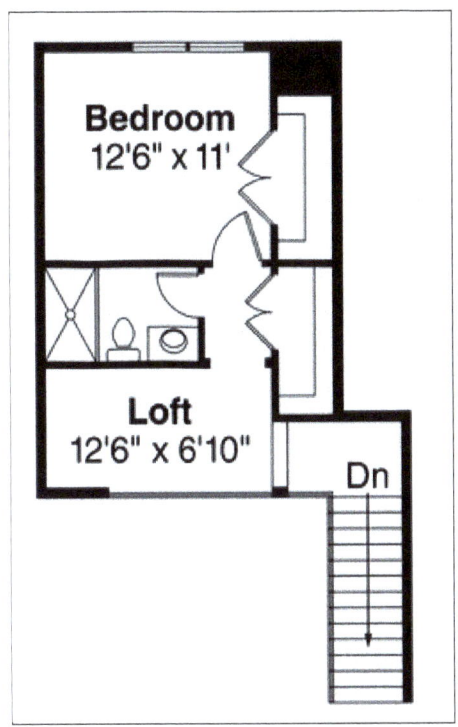

Upper Floor Plan for a Barndominium with Loft

This is a more contemporary take on the traditional barndominium facade.

This design embraces natural light in its entirety. This home maximizes open space to make it appear and feel much larger than it is, with large barn doors opening up from the great room and soaring ceilings throughout the common areas.

The main suite has an expansive walk-in closet and a large L-shaped bathtub in the en suite bathroom. Feel free to throw a dance party in your shower in the morning. We'll keep it a secret.

Floor Plan of a Barndominium with a Garage Apartment

Floor Plan of a Barndominium with a Garage Apartment - Front Exterior

If you or a family member is accustomed to apartment life but wants more room for work and creativity, this design would be an excellent choice for your first house. The ideal open space for a studio, workshop, or garage is available on the main level. The living area, which includes a kitchen, bedroom, banquette, and bathroom, is located just upstairs. You can put the days of apartments with a single closet behind you thanks to the ample storage space throughout.

Plan of the Duplex Barndominium

Floor Plan of the Duplex Barndominium - Front Exterior

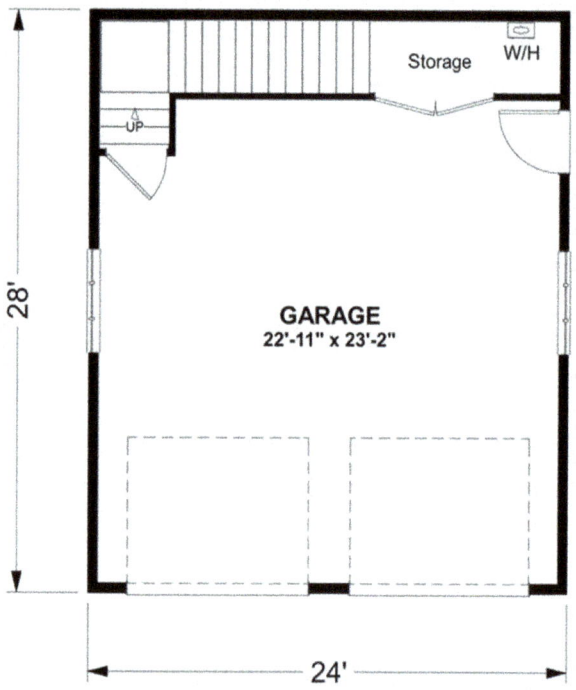

Main Floor Plan of a Barndominium with Garage Apartment

Upper Floor Plan of a Barndominium with Garage Apartment

This two-story barndominium floor plan, ideal for makers and craftspeople, is a fantastic illustration of how to maximize 562 sq. feet.

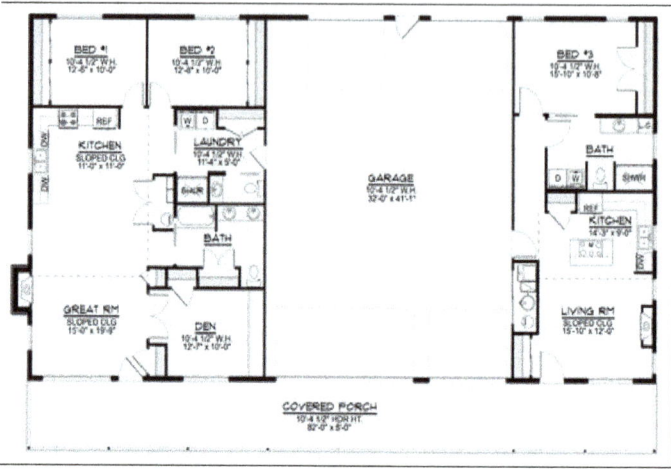

Floor Plan of Duplex Barndominium - Main Floor Plan

This floor plan for a barndominium is one of the most unusual designs we've seen yet. This one-story layout places a carport in the middle of the house to divide it into two independent living areas.

With a kitchen, a bathroom, and living and sleeping areas on both sides, this house is ideal for intergenerational households or for providing guests with a little additional seclusion. But fear not—a stunning covered porch that links the two living areas will ensure that you never lose contact with your loved ones.

Floor Plan of a Barndominium with a Courtyard

Floor Plan of a Barndominium with Courtyard - Front Exterior

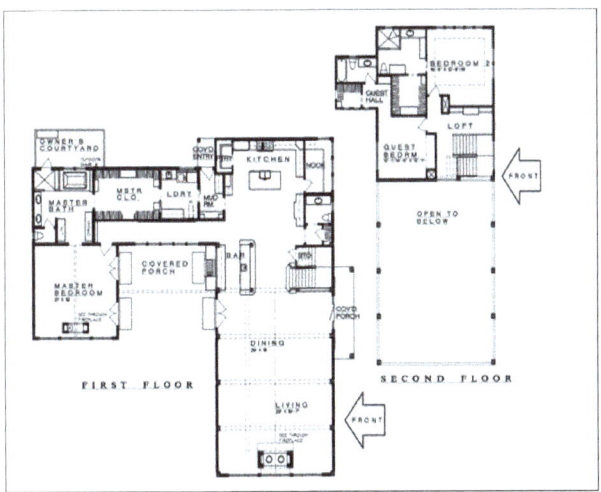

Main and Upper Floor Plans for a Barndominium with Courtyard

The floor layout for this opulent barndominium is what fantasies are made of. This house is among the most opulent on the list with its two see-through fireplaces, floor to ceiling windows, owner's patio, and tall vaulted ceilings.

The bar area is one of this design's most distinctive elements. This well-positioned bar is the ideal place to host friends if you're the kind of person who enjoys a more laid-back dining experience.

It's okay if your guests choose to stay overnight. Two additional bedroom suites are located in the loft just upstairs. This multifunctional space might easily be used as a private area for family members that require their own place, or as a home office.

Breezy Floor Plan for a Barndominium

Floor Plan for a breezy barndominium: Front Exterior

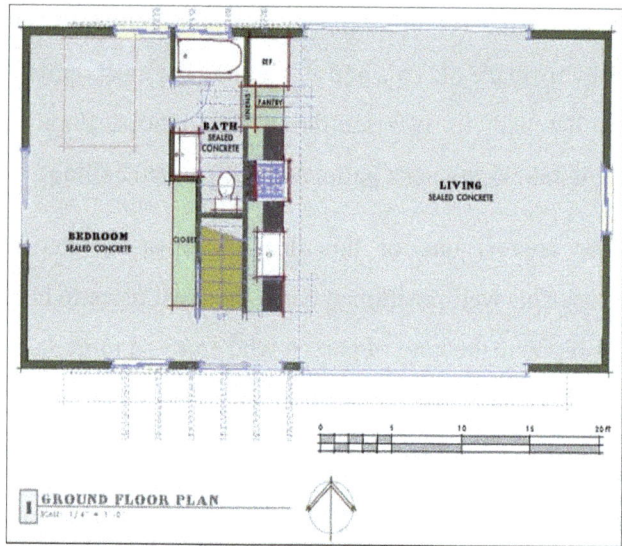

Main Floor Plan of the Breezy Barndominium Floor Plan

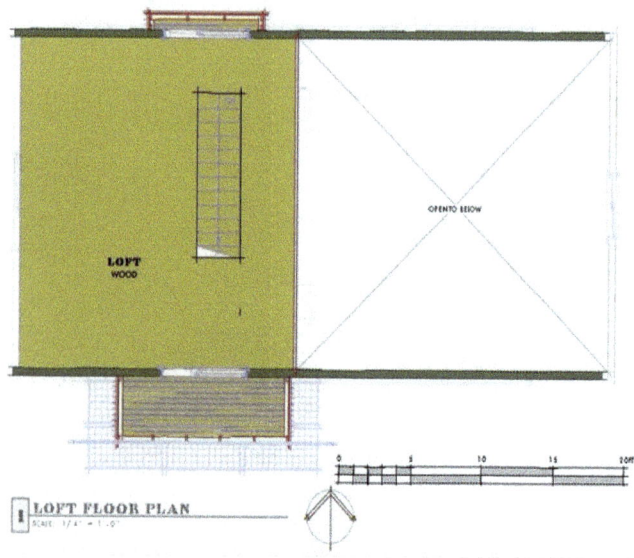

Floor Plan for Breezy Barndominium - Upper Floor Plan

If the residences on this list didn't resemble barns in some way, they wouldn't be referred to as barndominiums. But the best floor plan for maintaining the barn feel is this one-bedroom layout.

Despite having a barn-like appearance, this floor layout provides a special connection to the natural world. The entire living area of the house opens up to the outside through large barn doors on either side. This smart design ensures that cool summer breezes reach every nook of the house. Use the balcony off the upper loft on chilly evenings.

Floor Plan of a Barndominium with Outdoor Space

Front exterior floor plan of a barndominium with outdoor space

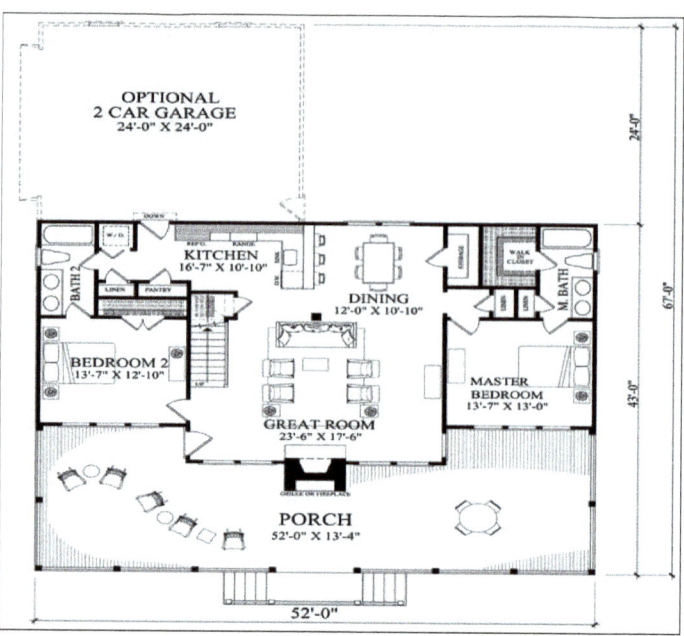

Main Floor Plan of a Barndominium with Outdoor Space

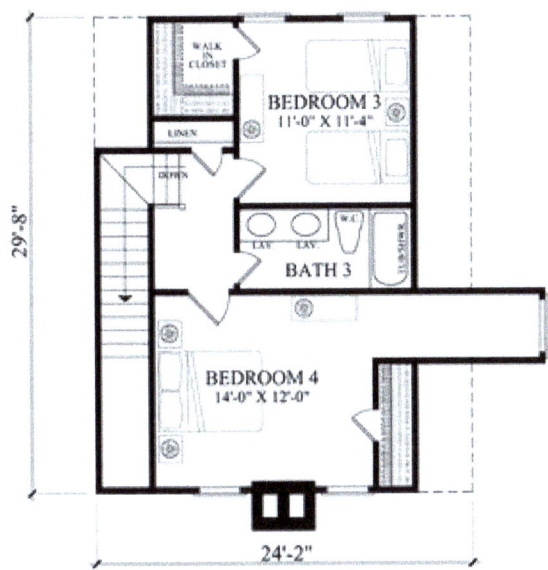

Open Concept Floor Plan for a Barndominium - Front Exterior

Upper Floor Plan of a Barndominium with Outdoor Space

The traditional covered porch is elevated to a whole new level by this inventive design. This chic outdoor area is a terrific way to extend the great room and keeps cozy on chilly evenings thanks to the fireplace in the middle.

This floor plan, with the main and guest suites on either side, was created with the intention of creating a gathering place at the center of the house.

Two separate bedrooms are available on the upper floor for visitors and family members who require a little extra privacy. One of the bedrooms has a comfortable extended nook that would be ideal for a window seat or modest reading nook.

Open Floor Plan for a Barndominium

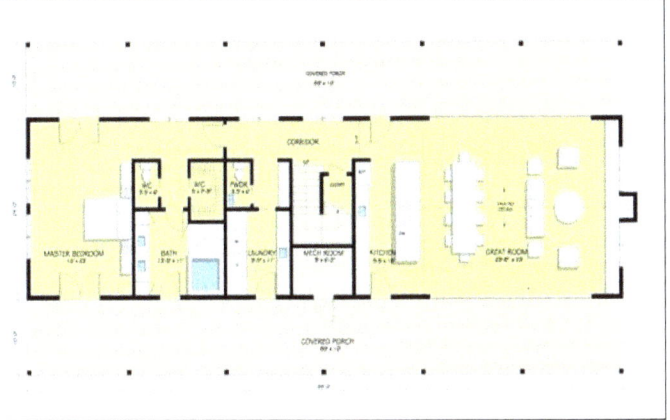

Main Floor Plan for a Barndominium with an Open Layout

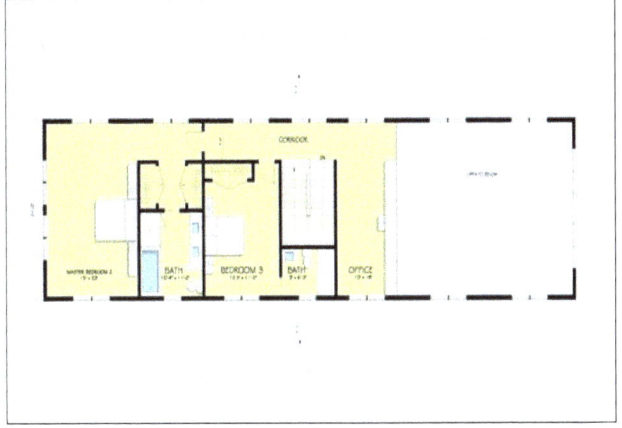

Open Floor Plan for a Barndominium: Upper Floor Plan

Not to mention, this two-story barndominium floor plan has a contemporary style that maintains everything tidy, clean, and easy to use.

The most striking aspects of this floor plan are undoubtedly the enormous covered porches on both sides and the high ceilings in the great area. But if you examine a little more closely, you'll see that every component of this house has been carefully chosen.

The office area that faces the expansive great room ensures that you never miss a "dinner's ready!" moment." A summons from below. You can easily reach the long porches from every room on the main floor, which allows you to take advantage of the opportunity to breathe in some fresh air while heading to the laundry room or kitchen.

How many different kinds of basements can a barndominium have?

Barndominiums can have the same kinds of basements that regular houses do, such as

- Partially finished basements
- Walk-out basements
- Completely finished basements

Most basement walls are made of concrete, and the floors may also be made of concrete. In a full basement, the floor is the same size as the building's frame. It takes up the same space as the first floor, the basement.

Post frames or steel frames are used to build normal barndominiums. The post columns are anchored in the ground. If there is a full basement, the posts might need to be attached to frames on top of the crawl space. This isn't a big change in the building process, but it's still best to work with a builder who has done this before.

Having a partial basement is an easy way to do it. Some basements only go below a certain part of the house. A piece of concrete holds up the rest of the first floor. It is cheaper and easier to build a half basement than a full basement in a barndominium.

The frame is still being built in the same way because the perimeter of the house is still held by the concrete slab. The downside is that you won't get as much extra room.

An choice that is the most difficult to build is a walk-out basement, which is usually only used on properties that have a slope or hill. Because the base is sloped, the back end is at ground level, so you can add a door. However, this choice costs more because it is harder to use.

Basements are good for barndominiums for these reasons:

There are many benefits to adding a basement floor to a barndominium, such as making the space bigger. Bottom floors are often used for storage, cleaning, or extra living space. If you have a small lot and need a small floor plan, extra square footage could help.

Basements also keep you safe. The walls of the house made of concrete are safer than the frame made of wood or steel. You can hide out in the basement during bad weather or storms.

It is usually much cooler in the basement than on the top floors because it is built below the ground. If you're going to be making your barndominium in a hot area, a basement can help you cool off.

What's Wrong with Basements for Barndominiums

Cost is one of the main problems with adding a basement below a barndominium. Getting the ground ready for the basement and paving the walls with concrete takes time, work, and supplies.

The price of basement foundations for a full or partial basement is about $33 per square foot. Crawl rooms cost around $13 per square foot on average. The cheapest choice is a concrete slab, which costs only $7 per square foot.

It also takes less time to make a concrete slab. If the barndominium floor plan is big enough, you might only have to wait a few days or up to two weeks for a basic slab. It might take a few weeks to finish a full basement.

Additionally, remember that a basement is not always a replacement for living room above ground. Basement rooms aren't officially bedrooms in most places unless they have windows and doors that lead to the outside. Most of the time, this is only possible with a walk-out basement.

There may not be a lot of natural light in the room if you decide to use the basement as an extra living place. To live in the area, you might need to finish the walls, ceiling, and floors and add enough artificial lighting.

Other Choices for Barndominiums Besides Basements

You can choose between a block foundation or a crawl space if you don't want to install a basement foundation.

Most homes are built on slab foundations, which have a plain, flat cement slab. Because they are easier to make, you can start building the frame of the barndominium faster. Plus, slabs are the cheapest choice.

Crawl spaces are usually empty rooms that are only three to four feet high. Simply enough space to crawl. Crawl spaces are mostly used for extra storage and getting to the room under the floors.

As with a partial basement, a tunnel can be built with a slab around it to fit the barndominium frame. This way, the frame's design doesn't have to be changed.

Last Thoughts on Basements in Barndominiums

There are some good and bad things about barndominium basements. If you decide to add a basement, you will have to do more work to finish your new house. The due date could be pushed back by at least one month.

The job will also cost more if you add a basement, especially if you want to make it full or have a walk-out.

There are some problems with basements, but they are still useful adds to any barndominium. In addition to extra room, they let you set up your washer and dryer. You can even finish the inside of the basement to make a home theater or game room if it's big enough.

The bottom line is that barndominiums offer a lot of the same style choices as regular homes. You can have any kind of basement, but it might take more work and steps. If you want to add a basement, you might want to hire a builder who has done basement foundations before.

Getting the Barndominium Life Program is the best thing you can do if you want to learn more about barndominiums and the idea of a basement-equipped barndominium.

Chapter 8

Barndominium Garage Doors

Modern Aluminum Garage Doors were used to build a designer's dream home.

The breezeway runs down the middle of the building and has garage doors on both ends. These doors separate the space into a living wing and a shop/office wing. The breezeway and the living room can easily move from one to the other by opening a third garage door.

Kelly Moore, a photographer and artist, planned her dream home near West Monroe, Louisiana. She got ideas from three places: light, barns, and old dogtrot houses. She ended up with a beautiful "Barndominium," a famous new type of home that combines modern and rustic design to make a big barn-like building with a long, open breezeway that lets in lots of natural light and connects the indoors to the country. The Overhead DoorTM model 521 in Kelly's barn makes it big enough for her busy family of five, plus a guest bedroom and a shop for her husband. The barn is on 15 acres of land in the country in northern Louisiana.

There is a fourth door between the living room and the home's wrap-around patio that is made of metal. This lets Kelly's kids ride bikes and roller skate from the middle of the house to the outside, and it also makes the space brighter. In the open area, the family also holds events, tracks live music, and workshops.

The Overhead Door Modern metal Collection uses both glass and metal to make doors that look great, are strong, and let lots of light in. Modern garage doors are used by designers to make creative places better while also making them more useful. The doors' clean lines and sleek look make them appealing.

The Claim About Garage Doors

One of the most sought-after design features of a "barndominium" is often the cool, industrial glass garage doors that lead into the living area.

The Bad Things About Garage Doors:

I'll start with the bad things: having a garage door in your place isn't all sunshine and sparkles. A garage door has a few clear cons that I think people who are thinking about getting one should be aware of.

1) Cost: You can't just buy a glass garage door like you would any other garage door. Not if you want to follow the rules for building homes! Usually, your garage door needs to be specially made for a residential purpose because of two things:

-R Value: This tells you how well the door insulates, or stops heat from going through it. It must meet the "R Value" standards set by your building department for a home. You will need between R-13 and R-25 (non-ceiling), but this will depend on the zone. It is better to have a bigger R-Value. In addition to what a normal garage door (meant for a non-conditioned space) provides, the extra insulation usually needs to be made in a special way, which adds to the cost.

—**U-Value:** This is a number that tells you how well a window or glass blocks heat (that is, how much heat escapes through it). To get really technical, U-Value is found by dividing the rate at which heat moves through a substance (like a window) by the change in temperature across the structure of the window. It is more likely that heat will be kept in when the U-Value is low. Like R-Value, most garage doors aren't made to meet the U-Value building code for residential/conditioned spaces. This means they have to be custom made, which costs more.

2) Sealing: No matter who tells you that your garage door will seal along the bottom as well as a door with tracks (like a slide door), it's not true. It's not possible. We had seals made to fit our door and floors perfectly, and our slab was graded to fit the door opening. Other clients and homes have tried many other methods to get "the perfect seal," but none of them have worked.

What does that mean? That you have a huge hole that lets a lot of air, rain, or bugs in? NO! Homes can still be very energy efficient even if they have a glass garage door. You may see a few more bugs (rollie-pollies and pill bugs are the worst offenders), but nothing too scary or gross. But keep in mind that it won't close like a door with a track. The structure just doesn't allow it.

3) Privacy: The garage door is made of glass. Which means that anyone can see in, and you can't just go to Target and buy curtains to cover it. This doesn't really matter if you're building in the country, but it's still something to think about. You can also tint the glass, but that will change the color of the glass and the amount of light that comes in, which might not be what you want.

The Good Things About Garage Doors:

Now for the fun stuff. Yes, having a glass garage door in your living room is very nice. These are the pros we've found:

1. let in **natural light**. A wall of windows is the best way to enjoy your view or let in natural light. A glass garage door can let in more light and air and let you enjoy the view outside.
2. having a garage door in your living space is very **convenient**. This may sound silly, but moving big pieces of furniture is a breeze when you have one!

3. This is cool: we've rollerbladed from the patio to inside the house. When it rains in the summer, we open the door to enjoy the smell. When we have parties, people can easily move from the front yard to the living room. You can't argue with the

"coolness" of having a glass garage door in your house!

Finally, you should think about the pros and cons of each design element in your home and choose the one that best fits your budget, way of life, and style.

Chapter 9

Garage Plans with Barndominium Style

The barn-style doors, gable roofs, and country exteriors of these garage plans make us think of barndominium plans. Open floor plans inside give you a lot of room for cars, gardening tools, or anything else you can think of. There are also living areas in some plans, so these buildings can be used to house friends or family members. Take a look at these useful barndominium-style garage ideas.

Barn-style garage plan Plan 1070-120:

Farmhouse-Style Garage

Front View The farmhouse-style garage plan 1070-120 shows the main floor plan.

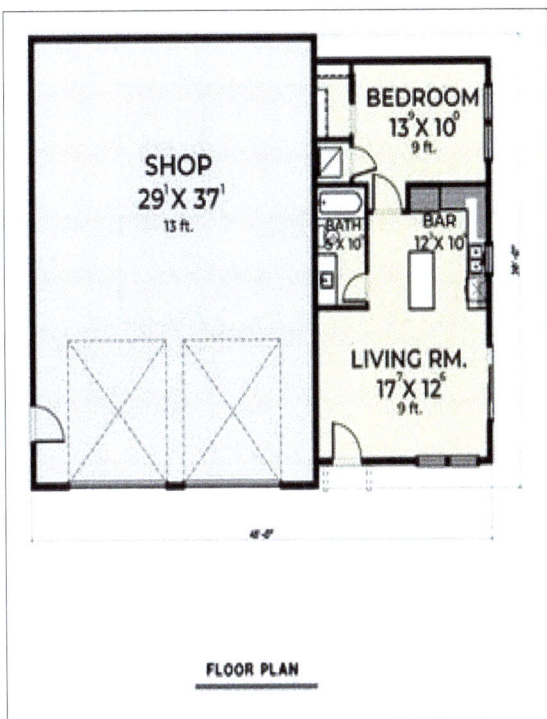

The left side of this flexible garage plan has more than 1,000 square feet of open space, which is more than enough room for two cars. The living room on the right leads into the living space of the building, which has a kitchen with a center bar, a bedroom with lots of closet space, and a full bathroom.

Garage That's 2,500 Square Feet Garage That's 2,500 Square Feet 1070-121

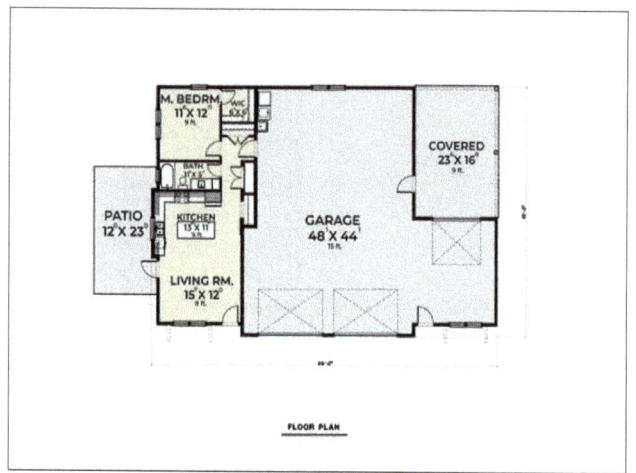

Front Outside 2,500-Sq.-Feet Garage 1070-121 - Main Floor Plan

This garage plan is definitely on the bigger side. The building is great for both storage and living, as it has a full apartment and a huge amount of room for parking or working. A handy apartment across the garage has a kitchen and living room that are open to each other, a main bedroom with a walk-in closet, and a full bathroom. Guests are also welcome to use the patio outside of this flat.

Country-Style Garage Plan

Country-Style Garage Plan 124-1052 - Front and Back

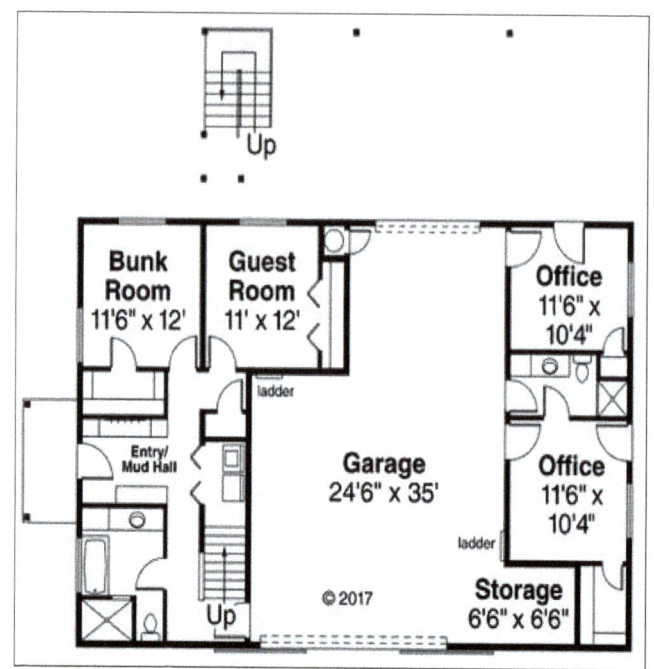

Garage Plan 124-1052 with a Country Style - Main Floor Plan

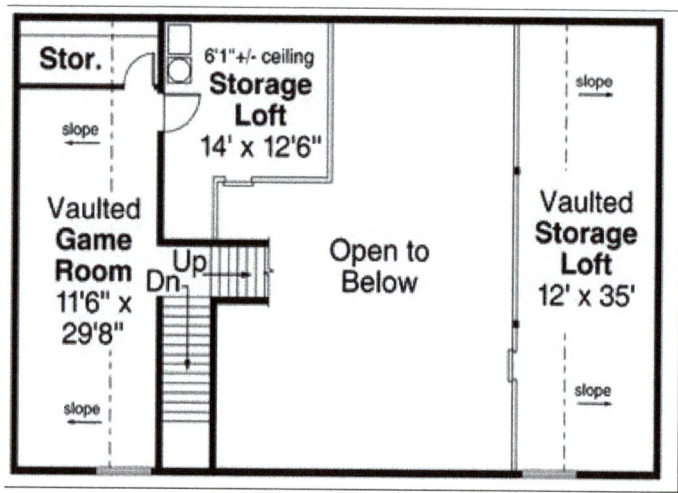

Garage Plan 124-1052 with a Country Style - Upper Floor Plan

With its red siding, barn doors, and dome topped with a wind vane, this garage plan looks like a classic barn from the outside. Inside, there is a large parking area and two different living rooms on either side. On the right, there are two offices next to each other and a full bathroom in the middle. This makes it possible for several people to work from home or for you to run a small business from your own home. The space has a mud hall, two bedrooms, and a full bathroom all around it. This makes it a comfortable place for people to stay. This is the vaulted game room and store space on the second floor. If you keep going up to the top floor, you'll find an apartment with a bedroom suite, a gallery-style living and dining room, and even a covered deck.

Flexible Plan for a Country Garage

Flexible Country Garage Plan 1064-75 - Front and Back

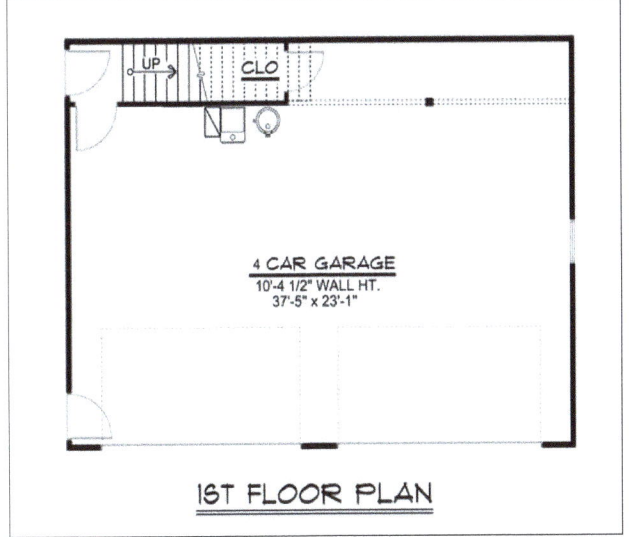

Main Floor Plan for Country Garage Plan 1064-75

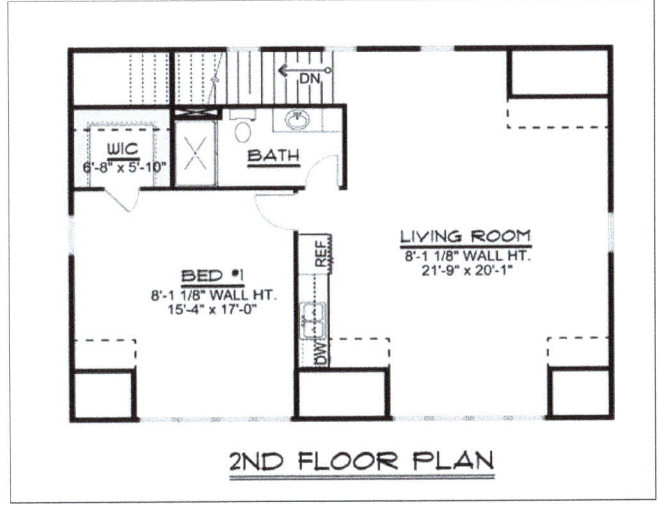

The 1064-75 country garage plan is flexible and has an upper floor plan.

On the main floor of this space, there is room for up to four cars, which is great for family vehicles or storing lawn tools or RVs. The second level is reached by steps and has a large living room that is great for hanging out with family or friends. There is a bathroom nearby and a walk-in closet in the bedroom, which is pretty big. This new, cozy addition is a great place for people to stay.

Plan for a farmhouse garage

Front and Back of Farmhouse Garage Plan 47-1090

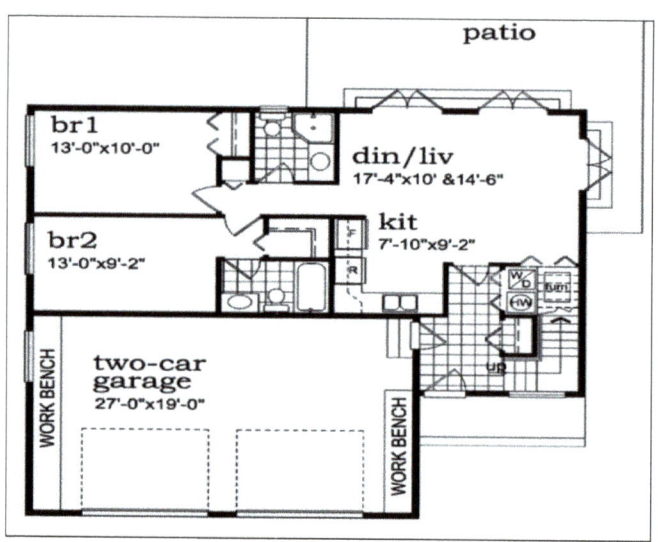

Plan 47-1090 for a farmhouse garage: main floor plan

Plan for a country garage The front of Country Garage Plan 932-91 Plan 932-91 for a country garage

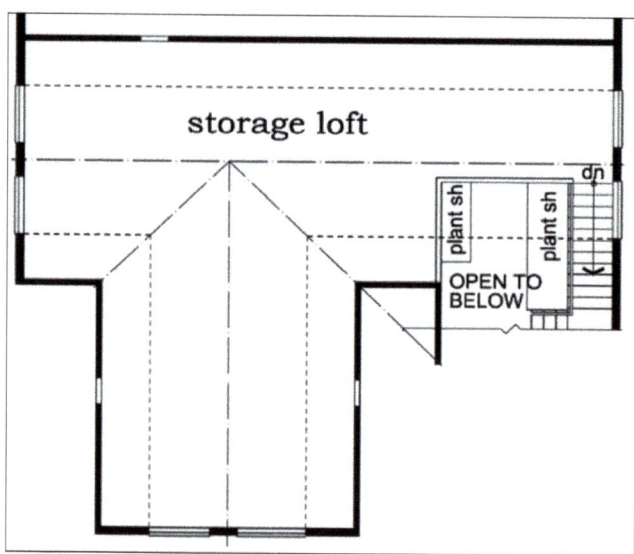

Garage Plan 47-1090, Inspired by a Farmhouse - Upper Floor Plan

This farmhouse-style garage plan has space for two cars at the front, with a table on each side. The living room and dining room that are joined in the back of the building are great for relaxing, and the laundry room and mudroom are close by for easy access. This level has two beds and two bathrooms, so guests can be alone. A storage room on the second floor could help you keep your things in order.

Country Garage Plan

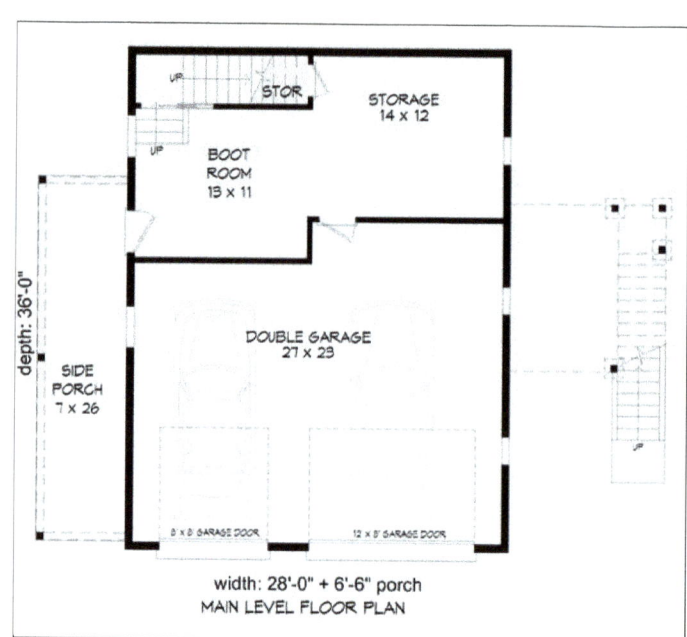

main floor plan Plan 932-91 for a country garage

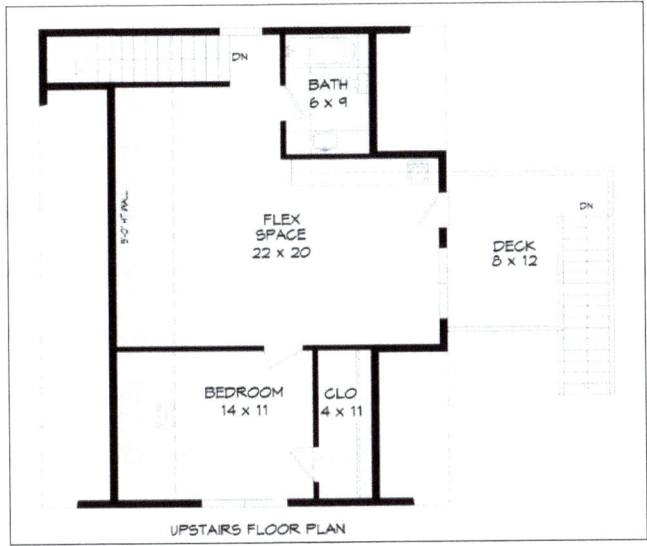

upper floor plan

This barndominium plan is great for people who want to make the most of their living and storage area. Part of the bottom level is a garage that can fit two cars. There is a separate room for boots and storage in the back to keep the space clean. There is a large open space upstairs that goes to the deck on the second floor. This area is surrounded by a bedroom with a large closet. With a full bathroom on this level, the second level of this barndominium-style garage plan can be used as a great guest apartment.

Rustic garage Plan

Plan for a rustic garage Plan 117-483 for a rustic garage

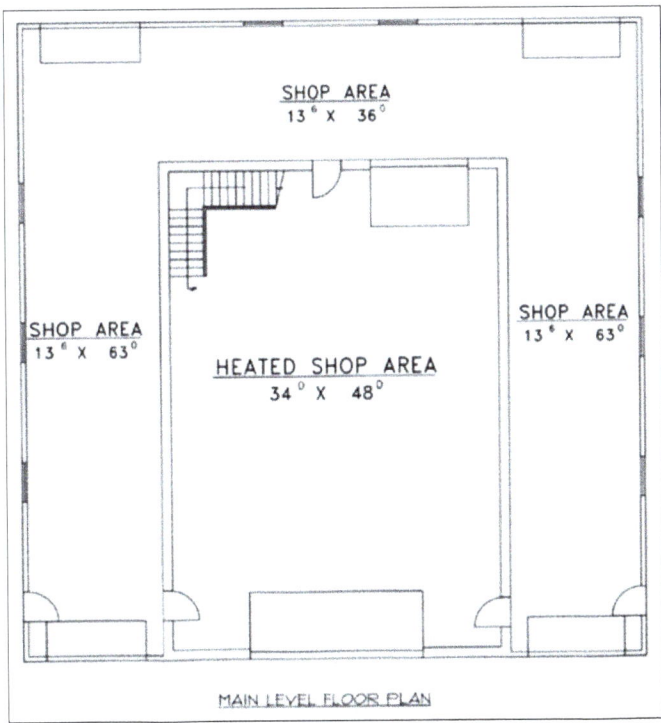

front and back views the main floor plan for the rustic garage plan 117-483

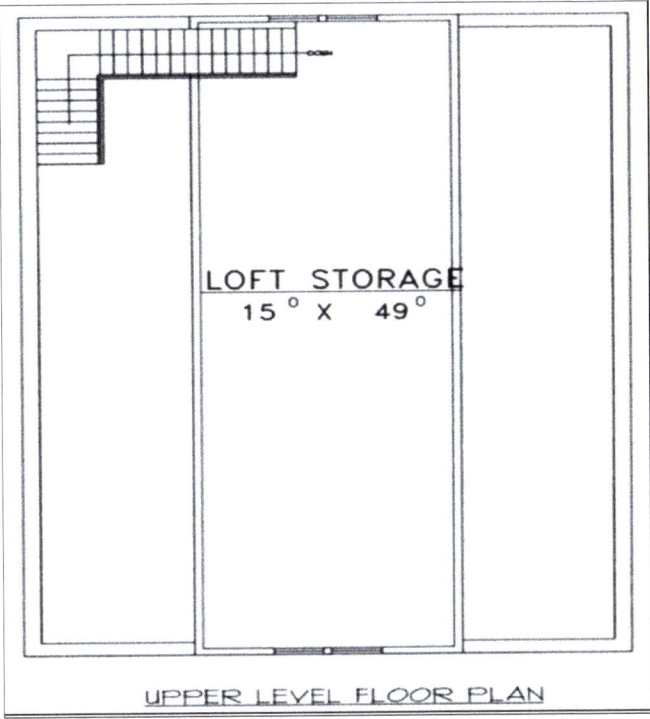

Plan 117-483 for a rustic garage on the second floor

Need a lot of parking spots? The gambrel roof on this one-of-a-kind plan makes me think of old-fashioned barn style. Inside, there is a heated shop area big enough for a car, and on three sides there is more shop room or parking. If you love making things, this main level is perfect for you because it has lots of room to work. This rustic, barndominium-style garage plan makes the most of every square foot by including a big loft space on the second floor for easy storage.

Classic Barn-Style Garage

A traditional barn-style garage Traditional Barn-Style Garage 124-1098

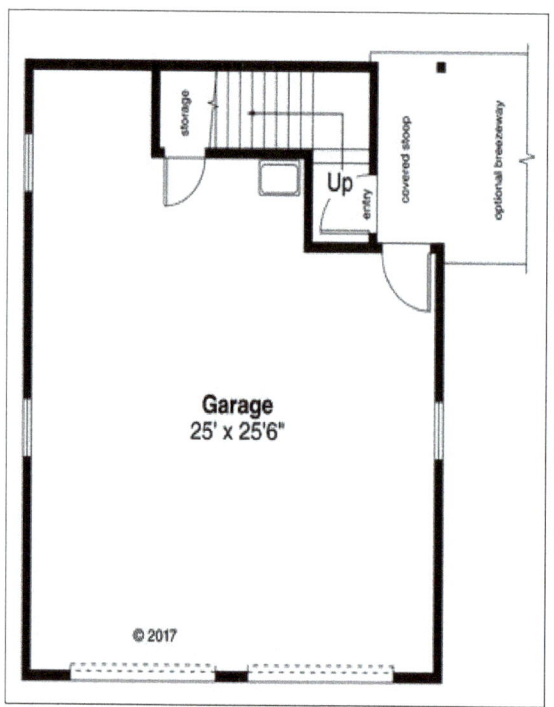

Front View The main floor plan for the classic barn-style garage 124-1098

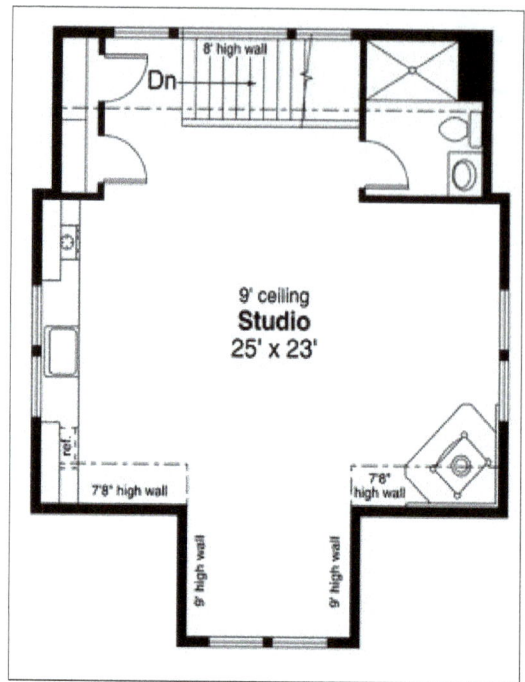

Garage in the Style of a Classic Barn 124-1098 - Upper Floor Plan

The upper level of this building has more than 600 square feet of room, so it's ready to be your home office, studio, or anything else you need. Up here, there is a full bathroom that makes it easy to take a break from talks.

What's the Difference Between a Pole Barn and a Barndominium? Three Good Reasons Why It's Better to Have Living Space and Storage in One Building

Do you want to build a pole barn or a barndominium? Use this comparison to find out what's good and bad about each choice. To begin with, let us talk about what barndominiums are.

The same kind of building methods are used to make barndominiums as for pole barns. The first barndominiums were actually built out of old barns on a horse ranch. Since the 1930s, stable houses and other farm buildings have been built quickly with pole framing, also known as post-frame construction. Real estate developers chose to turn horse barns into living spaces because the barns are stable.

In the 1980s, the first barndominiums were built. After many years, barndominiums are now a popular choice instead of regular houses. You might not need to build a separate pole barn if you build a barndominium.

What's the Difference Between a Pole Barn and a Barndominium?

There is a type of house called a barndominium that is built the same way pole barns are. Big poles that are put deep into the ground are used to build a pole barn. The poles hold up the walls and top, making the inside big enough to house and feed animals.

That pole frame helps you build tall buildings with only one floor. The ceilings of most barns are 12 feet high, while the ceilings of most homes are 8 or 9 feet high. There may also be a loft or mezzanine room in the upper part of the barn.

The frame of a barndominium is a lot like the frame of a pole barn. But a base is poured first, before the frame is built. A lot of barndominiums are made on slabs of concrete. To make the frame more stable, the poles or posts are attached to the base.

The inside is the biggest difference between a pole barn and a barndominium. There are bedrooms, bathrooms, a kitchen, a dining room, and a living room inside a barndominium that has been built to look like a house.

The plumbing, electrical, and heating systems in barndominiums are the same as those in regular houses. A boiler keeps the house warm in the winter, and a water heater heats water for use. Pole barns are usually not heated unless animals or tools need to be kept at a certain temperature.

Why You Should Build a Pole Barn

A pole barn is usually built to give you extra room for a certain reason. A pole barn is often used for:

- Housing animals
- Storing tools and other things
- Keeping hay dry
- Meet-ups
- Garages
- Places to store things
- Fun Things

If none of these things are why you need extra room, you might be better off building a barndominium instead. A pole barn, on the other hand, is a cheap and easy way to add a building with a roof to your land.

It's easy and cheap to build a pole barn. You can expect to pay between $15,000 and $30,000 for a pole barn if you hire a builder. Do-it-yourself projects start at around $4000. Building something usually costs between $20 and $35 per square foot. A wood-stud frame can cost around $10 per square foot, while the frame itself may cost around $8 per square foot.

Why You Should Build a Barndominium

If you want to build a pole barn, it's likely because you need more room than a regular wood home can give you. You can get the room you need and a place to live in a barndominium. A barndominium is basically a big pole barn that has been finished on the inside. On the other hand, some of the inside may not be finished.

The barndominium's open part can be used in the same ways as a pole barn. The area can be used as a workshop or to store things or animals.

You get a connected barn, which has a number of benefits:

- Simple to get to
- Better control of costs
- Making better use of land

It is helpful to build a house with a barn or work area connected. You don't want to go outside to get to the barn from your house. Depending on how the barndominium is set up, there may be a door or hallway that leads from the living area to the barn room. If you want to build a barndominium, you can find floor plans online, use tools to make your own design, or give your drawings to a professional.

It is also less expensive to build a barndominium than to build a pole barn and a separate house. You can build the space you need with just one crew, so you don't have to pay for two different ones. If you compare this to building each structure individually, it should save you time and money. Even though it serves two purposes, a barndominium costs less to build than a regular house.

A barn that is attached to your house is also a better use of the space you have. Putting two different buildings together takes up more land than putting them together as one. You can add on to your land in the future if you use less of it now. Now that you know these things, you need to plan even more for your barndominium's funding and insurance.

Which Should You Build: A Pole Barn or a Barndominium?

For those who are happy with their home and only need room, a pole barn is the best way to go. With the right help, a pole barn can be put up in a few days.

Building a barndominium might be a good idea if you need room for storage in a pole barn but also want to make your living area look better. For people who may need a new home in the future, building a barndominium is a cost-effective choice. For instance, you might have an old home.

A brand-new house can be built that has both living space and a barn. You don't have to build two different buildings; you can just build one. Building a barn and a new house at the same time might take more time and cost more money.

Still, not everyone should build a barndominium. It's possible that you'd rather keep your barn and house separate than combine them into one building. Keeping the barn away from your house, for instance, keeps animals or a workplace from making noise. The noises from the barn might not bother people in the house.

Pole barns are usually made to store things or give animals a place to live. Barndominiums are homes, but they might have room that could be used for the same thing as a pole barn.

Building a pole barn could help you get more room if you already have a house. You could build a barndominium if you want a new house and a pole barn.

Chapter 10

How To Budget For Building A Barndominium

After that, we'll assist you with cost estimation and budget creation, covering building, site preparation, and interior finishing costs. Go ahead and research funding alternatives and cost-cutting techniques for building projects. You will be well equipped to start your barndominium journey by the end of this book!

Knowing What Barndominiums Are

A residential structure that blends living spaces with a barn or workshop is called a barndominium. In recent years, this unusual combination of spaces has become more and more popular, especially in rural areas, because of its cost, adaptability, and durability.

An explanation and idea

Words "barn" and "condominium" are combined to form the term "barndominium," but the term doesn't just refer to the combination of barn features; other useful spaces like workshops, garages, or even offices can also be included.

Large windows that let in plenty of natural light, high ceilings, and an open floor plan are common features of barndominiums. Often, the outside is composed of metal, which is weather-resistant and requires little upkeep. The user can decorate the interior in any style they choose, from a classic rustic look to a sleek modern industrial look.

Barndominiums are a unique experience that may be had by anyone seeking something new or needing a dedicated space for business or hobbies in place of standard stick-built dwellings.

Budget-friendly barndominium with a low price point.

Advantages of Constructing a Barndominium

Building a barndominium has a number of advantages, some of which are as follows:

1. Cost-Effectiveness: Because barndominiums can be built faster and with fewer materials than standard residences, they are frequently less expensive to build. Because metal resists rot, rust, and insect infestation, it can significantly lower maintenance expenses.
2. Energy Efficiency: The superior insulating qualities of metal buildings can assist reduce the amount of energy needed for heating and cooling. Several owners of barndominiums also decide to incorporate energy-saving elements, such solar panels or geothermal heating systems, to lessen their impact on the environment and their utility expenses.
3. Durability: Compared to some standard stick-built homes, a well-built barndominium may survive severe weather and last a longer time. Additionally, metal construction provides superior defense against bugs, mildew, and fires.

4. Customizability: Homeowners can create their own living environment with a barndominium as a blank canvas. There are almost limitless alternatives when it comes to the arrangement of rooms and the installation of extras like porches or lofts.
5. Multi-Functional Spaces: A property can be used in more flexible ways when it combines residential and functional areas, such a workshop or barn. Homeowners can benefit from the ease of having these spaces linked to their property as well as the financial savings associated with renting additional workspace or storage.

Examples and Use Cases of Barndominiums

Barndominiums are available in a variety of sizes and shapes to suit a range of requirements and tastes. Several instances of barndominium applications comprise:

1. Hobby Farms: Due to their need for a combination of living space and useful spaces for their farming operations, hobby farmers are particularly fond of barndominiums. While the living rooms provide comfort and convenience, the connected barn can contain cattle, feed, and equipment.
2. Workshops or Garages: A barndominium design can be advantageous for people who require large workshop space for enterprises or hobbies. Owners of cars, woodworkers, or even small-scale manufacturers might discover that it is more economical and efficient to have a sizable, dedicated room linked to their home.
3. Multi-Generational Living: Families who desire a multi-generational living arrangement can find accommodations in a barndominium. Elderly family members can have separate living spaces constructed for them so they can maintain their independence and solitude while yet being near to their loved ones.
4. Holiday Houses: Some people construct barndominiums as holiday houses, frequently in isolated or rural areas where they may engage in outdoor pursuits like fishing, shooting, and ATV riding. In addition to offering a cozy place to live, these houses may store equipment and leisure vehicles.
5. Commercial Ventures: Barndominiums can also be used for businesses, such as studios or galleries for art, or as event spaces or B&Bs. The distinctive and adaptable area can be set up to support a variety of enterprises and draw clients searching for a distinctive experience.

Organizing Your Apartment

A hybrid residential and commercial building that combines parts of a barn and a condominium is called a barndominium. Originally intended for agricultural purposes, they have developed into adaptable, multifunctional areas that meet the needs of both living and working. Although designing and constructing a barndominium might be thrilling, it also calls for meticulous planning. This manual will assist you in planning and creating your ideal barndominium from beginning to end.

Identifying Your Objectives and Purpose

Identifying the intended function of your barndominium is essential before you start planning. This will specify the design considerations that must be made and assist you in making well-informed judgments during the planning phase. To help you choose the purpose of a barndominium, think about the following questions:

1. Which use will the space be for, residential or commercial? or the two?
2. Will it be big enough for a home workshop, office, or equipment storage for farmers?
3. What pastimes or events are planned for the area?
4. What particular demands or preferences do the residents of the residential area have? How many will reside there?
5. Are there any criteria for adaptation or accessibility when aging in place?
6. Will the area be used for hosting events or providing entertainment for visitors?

Your selections regarding the site, layout, materials, finishes, and any legal or regulatory requirements will all be influenced by your understanding of your purpose and aims.

Choosing an Appropriate Location

Choosing the ideal site for your barndominium is essential to its planning. This could be a plot of property you want to buy or an existing piece of land you own. When selecting the ideal location, bear the following points in mind:

1. Land size: Verify that the plot has enough space for parking, storage, landscaping, and any other outside features, as well as your preferred barndominium size and style.
2. Topography: Slopes or uneven terrain may call for extra engineering and affect the price of building. Think about how the building will blend in with the surrounding environment.
3. Access to utilities: Look into the presence and accessibility of gas, water, sewage, and electrical connections.
4. Transportation and access: Make sure the plot has easy access to major thoroughfares, particularly for businesses or equipment transportation.

Creating a Layout for Your Barndominium

After deciding on the site and goal, start planning the physical configuration of your barndominium, paying attention to flow, aesthetics, and practicality. You can choose from one of the floor plans, work with an architect, or have BarndoPlans.com modify an already-existing floor plan. Important design components to think about are:

1. the quantity and size of living areas, bedrooms, and bathrooms in residential buildings.
2. The size of commercial or multipurpose spaces, like garages, workshops, and storage rooms.
3. Space division: How will the residential and commercial sections coexist? Open concept vs. separate rooms.
4. windows and doors positioned to maximize views, ventilation, and natural light.
5. potential for growth or flexible designs for upcoming need.

Selecting Finishes for the Interior and Exterior

The finishes you choose will have a big impact on how your barndominium looks and feels overall. Considering the goal, way of life, and individual preferences, take into account the following:

1. External materials: Wood siding, stone, or brick are alternatives to the typical steel or metal panels.
2. Roofing: Select from a range of materials, hues, and designs to guarantee longevity and sufficient storm defense.
3. Flooring: Choose sensible, low-maintenance materials like tile, luxury vinyl, or concrete.

4. Choose the materials and design for the built-in storage, kitchen, and bathroom cabinets and countertops.
5. Electrical and lighting: Choose outlets and lighting fixtures based on your demands, both functionally and aesthetically.
6. Insulation and energy efficiency: To preserve comfort and save utility expenses, design a suitable insulation system.

Comprehending Local Construction Codes and Standards

Finally, get knowledgeable about the zoning laws, building rules, and any required permissions that pertain to the construction of barndominiums in your area. While certain jurisdictions may have regulations on land usage, building size, setbacks, and other features of your design, keep these things in mind during the planning phase. Adherence to established norms and guidelines will guarantee a seamless building procedure and alleviate possible legal complications.

To manage these restrictions, get help from a local compliance officer, architect, or builder. Engage with your neighbors and local community as well to maintain good connections both during and after construction.

Building a new home or starting a large renovation project can be expensive, so budgeting and cost estimation are essential when planning a barndominium. However, with the right planning, research, and careful consideration, you can design the ideal space that meets your particular needs and preferences. The many facets of estimating construction costs, including site preparation and land development costs, utility installation and connection fees, interior finishing prices, and factoring in additional expenditures and contingencies, will all be covered in this book.

Creating a Budget and Estimating Expenses

How to Compute Construction Costs

Consider the following elements to determine an accurate cost estimate for building your new home:

Materials: Siding, Roofing, Insulation, and Structure

A sizeable amount of your cash will go toward the materials for your home's structural elements, which include the roofing, siding, insulation, foundation, and frame. The size and kind of construction (steel or wood frame, for example), the materials utilized, and local prices can all have a significant impact on material costs. To obtain an exact quotation for these essential construction components, be ready to investigate suppliers and contractors.

Costs of Labor and Expert Services

Your building budget will also consider the cost of labor and expert services. Their prices can vary based on their level of skill, the complexity of the project, and local labor rates. These fees apply to designers, architects, general contractors, and subcontractors (which include people or teams who specialize in particular construction jobs, such framing, plumbing, and electrical work). Budgeting for the permits, inspections, and compliance certifications that local building authorities require is preferable.

Including Land Development and Site Work Costs

The expenditures of grading, excavating, and site preparation are included in site work and land development charges. These costs quickly add up, especially in places with poor soil conditions or steep slopes. Costs for site enhancements like retaining wall, driveway, or sidewalk construction may also apply. It's also critical to account for any costs associated with stormwater management, erosion control, and environmental preservation that may be mandated by municipal laws.

Accounting for Connection and Installation Fees for Utilities

Water, sewage, natural gas, and power utility lines may need to be extended or installed at a new construction site. Depending on your location, the needs of the utility company, and local laws, these fees may differ considerably. The project budget may be impacted by ongoing utility connection and service fees in addition to installation costs.

Taking Interior Finishing Costs Into Account

Paint, Textures, Flooring, and Drywall

The price of interior finishing includes all materials—from flooring to paint and drywall—as well as any unique treatments or finishes. The cost of these materials varies greatly depending on the intended style and feel; custom or high-end materials can drastically increase prices, while basic paint and flooring options are more affordable.

HVAC, electrical, and plumbing systems

The complete plumbing, electrical, and HVAC (heating, ventilation, and air conditioning) system installation and setup are extra costs that can complicate your budget. These expenses can also vary greatly based on the appliances and fixtures selected, the caliber of the materials, and the required degree of energy efficiency.

Keeping in Mind Extra Costs and Backup Plans

Any extras, such outdoor kitchens, swimming pools, or landscaping, as well as any modifications to the appliances, lighting, or cabinetry, should be factored in when creating your building budget. The budget should also take window treatments, furnishings, and other finishing touches into consideration.

Finally, make backup plans at all times. Unexpected events such as supply chain disruptions or unpredictable weather can affect the project's budget and schedule. As a general guideline, you should budget for a contingency reserve equal to 10–20% of the predicted cost to make sure you have enough money to cover unforeseen costs.

How to Fund Your Project for a Barndominium

A barndominium project's funding needs to be carefully planned, researched, and understood in terms of available financing choices. Investigating several funding options and carefully preparing your loan application and supporting materials are essential. To help you obtain the best financing terms for your barndominium project, this book will offer insights into documentation, negotiating tactics, financing possibilities, and interest rate considerations.

Examining Available Financing

When funding a barndominium project, there are a number of lending options to consider, such as home equity lines of credit (HELOCs), construction loans, mortgages, and personal loans. There might be further funding options available.

Loans for construction and mortgages

For funding your barndominium project, a construction loan or a normal mortgage can be a great choice. Usually, a mortgage pays for the cost of labor, building supplies, and site acquisition. The actual construction of the barndominium may be financed by a construction loan, which, when the project is finished, can be changed into a conventional mortgage.

Compared to mortgages, construction loans often have higher interest rates and may need a larger down payment percentage of the estimated total loan value. They do, however, provide flexible terms and funding availability throughout the building phase.

To select the best mortgage or construction financing for your barndominium project, it is imperative that you investigate several lenders and loan packages.

Credit lines for home equity (HELOCs)

If you currently own your home, or a sizable piece of the equity in it, and you haven't sold it yet, home equity lines of credit (HELOCs) may be a convenient option to fund your barndominium project. With this kind of loan, you can borrow money against the value of your house, frequently at a cheaper interest rate than you would pay on a conventional mortgage or construction loan. There's a chance you could save money on taxes by deducting interest from a home equity loan.

A draw term, during which you can access cash as needed, and a repayment period are typically associated with HELOCs. Remember that your house's value will determine how much you can borrow, and speak with your lender to learn about the terms and conditions of a home equity loan (HELOC).

Loans for Personal Use and Other Alternative Funding

Another alternative for funding a barndominium project is a personal loan, particularly if you have a good credit history and a steady source of income. Budgeting might benefit from the predictability that these loans' set interest rates and payback schedules often offer.

On the other hand, personal loans could have lower lending limits and higher interest rates than mortgages or home equity line of credit (HELOC). As a result, they could be better suited as an additional funding source or for smaller barndominium projects.

Other non-traditional funding options include crowdsourcing, loans from friends and family, and government subsidies and incentives for ecological or energy-efficient building techniques.

Getting Documentation and Loan Applications Ready

It's time to get your loan application and supporting paperwork ready after looking into your financing possibilities and deciding on a good kind of loan. Be ready to present financial documentation, including evidence of income, outstanding obligations, and assets. It can also be necessary for you to submit particulars regarding the barndominium project, like building contracts or architectural drawings.

Gather all required documentation and make sure it is correct, current, and well-organized. Discuss the requirements for your application with the lender of your choice, and be ready to submit any further information or supporting documentation they might ask for.

Haggling over Loan Terms and Interest Rates

In order to keep expenses down and guarantee long-term financial stability, it is essential to negotiate the best interest rates and loan terms for financing your barndominium project. Do some research on current market interest rates and learn about the offerings from different lenders before you begin negotiating.

Your eligibility for a certain interest rate will be greatly influenced by your credit score, down payment amount, and general financial situation. While keeping in mind the conditions of the loan, such as the length of the repayment term and any early penalties, aim for the lowest rates.

Never be scared to approach other lenders to compare offers or to ask for better loan terms. To assist you in negotiating the best financing conditions for your barndominium project, it could also be helpful to speak with a mortgage broker or financial advisor.

Tips for Staying on Budget During Construction

Collaborating with Reputable Experts

Working with dependable pros is one of the most crucial suggestions for staying within your construction budget. This involves working with a trustworthy architect, general contractor, and other subcontractors. It is essential to request numerous bids and evaluate the experience, credentials, and references of each candidate before choosing a professional for your job. Furthermore, confirm that they are licensed and insured for the particular work at hand.

Your building project's ultimate success depends on your choice of skilled personnel. Experienced groups with a track record of success can offer a trustworthy estimate and work well together to control expenses and prevent delays in the project schedule. For this reason, devoting time to team selection and research is essential to guaranteeing a more seamless and economical building process.

Monitoring Progress and Expenses Frequently

Maintaining financial stability while building necessitates careful observation of expenditures and developments. This entails regular site visits and thorough progress reports that account for all project-related expenses, including personnel and materials. Being actively involved will help you minimize financial risks and stay within your budget by allowing you to make necessary revisions to the construction design.

Setting up a method for monitoring spending and comparing it to the original budget is also essential. This entails scheduling frequent budget reviews, which may be conducted on a weekly or monthly basis based on the project's complexity and length. These assessments will assist you in finding any spending patterns or disparities that may require attention in order to keep your financial objectives on track.

Continuing to Communicate Effectively with Contractors

Budget management in construction requires effective communication. This entails keeping in close contact with your contractors and subcontractors to guarantee that all parties are aware of the project's deadlines, expectations, and financial limitations. To share project updates and resolve any issues, schedule frequent meetings or conference calls. Promote candid and open communication among team members.

Furthermore, having precise contractual agreements that specify the work to be done, when payments are due, and how change orders are handled will help reduce misunderstandings and disagreements and save you time and money when it comes to dispute resolution. A strong corporate culture and open lines of communication will help you better manage changes and avert possible budget overruns.

Value Creation and Cost-Reduction Techniques

Value engineering and cost-cutting techniques are useful tools for managing building budgets. Value engineering is the process of locating places where expenses can be cut without compromising the project's functionality or end quality. This could entail using prefabricated parts, looking for substitute materials, and expediting the building process.

Using volume discounts and bulk purchases to negotiate cheaper material costs is an additional tactic. Make sure you thoroughly weigh the financial effects of every design feature, and be ready to decide which ones may be changed to stay within your budget.

Getting Used to Unexpected Obstacles and Delays

Any construction project will often encounter unforeseen difficulties and delays, so being adaptable and flexible is essential to remaining under budget. This entails foreseeing possible problems and creating backup strategies to deal with them. Unexpected site circumstances, a lack of workers, problems getting permits, or delays in material delivery are a few examples of these difficulties.

It's critical to respond rapidly to unforeseen interruptions and modify project expectations accordingly. This may entail going over the budget again and redistributing funds to address fresh challenges. You may lessen the impact of unforeseen difficulties on the price and schedule of your project by managing them proactively, which will eventually guarantee a successful and economical building process.

What aspects need to be taken into account while creating a barndominium budget?

Think about things like the cost of the property, the building supplies, the permissions, the style, and the design when making a barndominium budget. Don't forget to factor in costs for labor, utilities, exterior and interior finishes, and any other customizations.

How much will it cost to create a barndominium in total?

Estimate the price per square foot, taking into account the costs of construction and customization, in order to get the overall cost. Next, figure out how big the ideal barndominium should be in square footage. Lastly, multiply the total square footage by the price per square foot.

Is it possible to lower the price of constructing a barndominium?

It is possible to cut costs by using energy-efficient materials, going with a more straightforward design, purchasing a prefabricated building kit, or thinking about doing some of the work yourself. To locate the greatest deal, compare costs and get bids from several contractors.

What elements affect a barndominium's cost per square foot?

The intricacy of the floor plans, the type of foundation, local labor expenses, and unique features like fixtures and finishes, as well as extra upgrades like energy-efficient windows and insulation, all have an impact on the cost per square foot.

How do financing alternatives and construction loans for establishing a barndominium operate?

Short-term loans used to finance the building process are called construction loans. Once construction is finished, they typically convert to a long-term mortgage with higher interest rates. Provide thorough building plans, estimates, and a clean credit history in order to be eligible for a construction loan.

Which licenses and regulations need to be taken into account when planning my barndominium budget?

Different licenses and costs can be necessary based on where you live. Permit prices are heavily influenced by local building, environmental, and zoning rules. Speak with the local government authorities to learn about the requirements and related expenses.